The Future of Europe

The Future of Europe: Reform or Decline

Alberto Alesina and
Francesco Giavazzi

The MIT Press
Cambridge, Massachusetts
London, England

MIT Press books may be purchased at special quantity discounts fro business or sales promotional use. For information, please email special_sales@mitpress. mit.edu or write to Special Sales Department, The MIT Press, 55 Hayward Street, Cambridge, MA 02142.

This book was set in Palatino by SNP Best-set Typesetter Ltd., Hong Kong and was printed and bound in the United States of America.

Library of Congress Cataloging-in-Publication Data

Alesina, Alberto.
The future of Europe : reform or decline / Alberto Alesina and Francesco Giavazzi.
    p. cm.
ISBN-13: 978-0-262-01232-4 (alk. paper)
ISBN-10: 0-262-01232-4 (alk. paper)
1. Europe, Western—Economic policy. I. Giavazzi, Francesco. II. Title.

HC240.A59944   2006
338.94—dc22

                                                                2006046203

10 9 8 7 6 5 4 3 2 1

to Rudi Dornbusch

Contents

Preface

We have been thinking about the issues discussed in this book for several years. We tackled them both in academic research and in articles published in several newspapers, by the two of us together and independently.

This book makes no pretense of being exhaustive. It is meant to be short and agile and directed to the general concerned public. In many ways each chapter could be a volume in itself. While we have tried to present our arguments carefully, we wanted to be brief even at the expense of being sometimes trenchant over subtleties and qualifications. The costs are obvious; the benefits, we hope, are the provocation and the incentive for the reader to react and even get mad!

Some of the ideas presented here stem from our academic research with other coauthors. We thank them for their invaluable contributions to our thinking; in particular, we thank Ignazio Angeloni, Robert Barro, Olivier Blanchard, Federico Etro, Alberto Giovannini, Edward Glaeser, Roberto Perotti, Bruce Sacerdote, Ludger Schucknecht, Enrico Spolaore, Guido Tabellini, and Romain Wacziarg. Many of these scholars also gave us comments on this manuscript: we are especially grateful to Olivier Blanchard. In addition to our coauthors listed above we wish to thank for comments Giuliano Amato, Franco Debenedetti, Angelo Cardani, Mario Draghi, Mario Monti, Andrei Shleifer, Guido Tabellini, Charles Wyplosz, and four anonymous referees for The MIT Press.

When we draw explicitly from our published research, we make the appropriate reference. Otherwise, we have chosen to write in a journalistic style that does not include explicit references to the literature. For assistance in assembling this manuscript we thank Ornella Bissoli, Amelia Spinelli, Alessandra Startari, and Yvonne Zinfon. Dana Andrus performed her usual great editing job.

The academic research from which many of these ideas were drawn was supported by National Science Foundation grants through the National Bureau of Economic Research (Alesina) and by grants from Bocconi University (Giavazzi).

Introduction

A recent poll taken in the European Union identified the United States as the biggest enemy of world peace, after Israel and North Korea, in that order. In the United States, anti-French sentiments are widespread. Cross-Atlantic relationships have rarely been at such a low point in the post–World War II era.

It would be superficial to attribute the cross-Atlantic animosity to the European aversion to the current American president, George W. Bush, or to the American irritation at the French and German opposition to the war in Iraq. The truth is that Americans and Europeans are different, think differently, and are becoming more different.

Europeans work less, take longer vacations, and retire early. Americans choose to work long hours. In August, Paris is a ghost town, except for the tourists, and Milan is a ghost town, period; in August, New York does not look very different than in any other month except for more European tourists. Europeans view job security and stability as a fundamental right and a ticket for happiness. Americans are willing to endure the ups and downs, the bankruptcies, and the unemployment spells as a necessary part of a market economy. Europeans tend to hold the same job for most of their life, Americans change jobs frequently. Europeans view any cut in the size of the welfare state as unacceptable. Americans view tax increases as an evil to be avoided at all cost. Europeans view inequality as a major problem. Inequality in the United States is on the rise, but Americans appear to be willing to live with it. Europeans believe that the use of force in international relations should almost never (read "never") be used. Americans believe in the relatively frequent use of force. Europe is relatively closed to foreign immigrants. America is a country of immigrants. Europeans believe that society determines much of an individual's fortune; Americans believe that individuals are responsible for their own fate. Americans believe that competition is critical for economic success and embrace it. Europeans are prompt to emphasize the benefits of a *Soziale Marktwirtschaft* (a social market economy), a model invented by Germany, which means putting restraints on market forces through government regulation.

These differences are becoming more, rather than less, deep-rooted. In the recent debate in France, ahead of the vote on the European constitution, both camps promised they would prevent the country from adopting a social system resembling the despised Anglo-Saxon "ultra liberalism." The American form of capitalism was the universal enemy; the disagreement was on the best way to fight it and be different. Any discussion about economic reform in Europe is prefaced by a disclaimer about the superiority of the European model compared to the American one. In the German election campaign of 2005, the conservative candidate, Angela Merkel, promised profound change but committed not to touch the basic characteristics of the German social model. All that her opponent had to do to avoid defeat was to scare German voters about the risks of market liberalism. By doing so, he engineered a phenomenal last-minute electoral turnaround. Americans, on the other hand, show no inclination toward changing their welfare system and making it more similar to the European one.

In this volume we discuss the problems that confront Europe using the rhetorical device of a comparison between Europe and the

United States along different dimensions. But this is not an academic book, and we are not shy in taking sides on the issues we analyze.

We are very critical of many aspects of the European model. But let us be clear. We do not argue that European countries should simply copy the United States and adopt identical policies. America is far from perfect; on the contrary, it has very serious problems. For instance, the American health care system is explosively expensive and many Americans do not receive adequate health care. American inner cities are an embarrassment, and the correlation between poverty and race is disturbing. America has a lot to learn from Europe. Some aspects of the European welfare state can ensure social solidarity and, when well designed, at relatively low efficiency cost.

Are we then saying that there is a "third way" in between the American model and the European model? No, or at least not in the common way in which this is understood. Those who argue that there is a third way—and talk about European reforms but in the next sentence emphasize that Europe should be different from the "American free market"—are simply fuzzy thinkers, the typical example being the German notion of a social market economy. A market economy is a market economy: qualifications are misleading. But, quite apart from blank and somewhat superficial endorsements of one model or another, our view is that Europe should adopt very large scale reforms that would make its markets and its institutions (such as universities and banks) look much more like those of the United States than they are now; of course, these reforms do not require the adoption of every aspect of, for instance, the American welfare system. The most important lesson that the United States can give to Europe is a belief that people respond to incentives and most of the time markets work, or at least they work better than any other mechanism.

Without serious, deep, and comprehensive reforms Europe will inexorably decline, both economically and politically. Absent profound change, in twenty or thirty years the share of Europe in the world economy will be significantly lower than it is today, and perhaps more important, its political influence will be much trimmed. Europeans seem to be living in the dream that their past splendor and their current prosperity cannot be lost. This is a mistake. A major European decline is indeed a serious possibility.

Think of Britain. It took the British people twenty years of economic and political decline to realize that their country was about to disappear from the world economic and political scene. In 1960, Britain's GDP per capita was 78 percent of US GDP per capita. By 1980, the ratio had fallen to 67 percent. Eventually Britain's decline was stopped by the policies adopted by Margaret Thatcher: by the beginning of the 1990s, the ratio of UK to US GDP per capita had stabilized to around 68 percent, although, relative to the United States, Britain never recovered the losses it suffered in the 1970s. (The percentages cited here are from Penn World Tables, compiled by the Center for International Comparisons of the University of Pennsylvania.)

Europe emerged from World War II with a level of per capita GDP that was less than half that of the United States: 42 percent. In the first thirty years after the war, Europe reduced that distance to one-half. By the end of the 1980s, its GDP per capita was 80 percent of the US level. Since then convergence has stopped. As a matter of fact in the last twenty yeas Europe has lost ground: GDP per capita today is about 70 percent of the US level, the position Europe had reached at the end of the 1970s. One is reminded of Britain in the 1970s, but we fail to see a new Mrs. Thatcher appearing on the European scene.

The prospect of an economic decline comes out sharper if one looks at individual countries. By 1970, Italy had reached a level of GDP per capita equal to 68 percent of the US level, a big achievement for a country that had started from 30 percent in 1950. By 1990, the ratio had reached 80 percent. Today, it is back to 64 percent, the level of the mid-1960s. In the same period, from the mid-1960s to today, the South Korean GDP per capita has risen, relative to the United States, from 12 to 50 percent. If the Korean GDP per capita keeps growing, relative to the United States, at the same rate it has grown over the past twenty-five years, by 2030, Korea will be richer than the United States. It is unlikely that this will happen: the Korean growth rate is, at least in part, the result of economic catch-up. The growth will inevitably slow down as Korea gets richer. But there is nothing that can automatically stop Italy's decline relative to the United States. If the relative decline continues at the current pace, in twenty-five years Italian GDP per capita will be one-third that of the United States. Relative to the United States, Italy will return to the conditions of the early 1950s. This doesn't mean Italy will be a poor country. The living standard of its (by then rather aged) citizens will continue to be good.

This raises the issue of whether relative economic decline is really so bad. In absolute terms, Europe is rich and it will not become poor overnight: the decline will be relative to other countries. Should Europeans care? To be concrete, why should a middle-class French-man be bothered if a middle-class tourist from Korea in Paris will soon be able to afford items out of reach for the French themselves? We believe that this hypothetical Frenchman should and would care. First of all, relative economic power matters in the area of interna-tional relations. Second, and perhaps more important, a host of eco-nomic and psychological research shows that individuals' happiness depends not only on their own income but also on their income rela-tive to others; it also depends on the growth of individual income. Third, societies that stop growing develop a "culture of stagnation," which can have a host of negative social consequences, a theme explored in a recent book by Harvard economist Benjamin Friedman. Sure our hypothetical Frenchman will enjoy his longer vacations and may criticize the hard-working Korean, but leisure increases happiness only to a point. In addition we should not forget that poverty has not been completely eradicated from Europe and a sustained rate of growth is the best cure for poverty. Generous welfare provisions become difficult to sustain in a slow growing economy.

In fact relative decline can turn into absolute decline. The experience of Argentina stands as a specter over Europe. At the beginning of the last century Argentina was among the richest countries in the world, twice as rich as Italy and about as rich as France. Then the world changed, but Argentineans kept thinking that exporting corn and beef was enough to remain rich. For a long time, until the crisis of 2001, most Argentineans were unaware of—or refused to recognize—the depth of their problem. When the crisis broke out all at once, Argentineans found themselves poor.

Are Europeans aware of these unpleasant possibilities? In our view, not entirely. But could they be right in not worrying? Certainly history suggests caution in making long-run predictions about winners and losers. In the late 1970s Japan was the model country and many thought that the United States was doomed: eventually exactly the opposite happened. In the same decade pundits were talking about the American decline, pointing to the TV images of long lines at the gas station, American hostages in Iran, and to the "irreversible" decline in American productivity. Today all of this seems far away—except, unfortunately, for hostages, although not in Iran. Will we be saying the same thing in twenty years about wrong predictions of European doom and gloom made in 2006? May be, but lacking comprehensive reforms, these gloomy predictions are likely to become true.

What happened to Europe? In the 1960s Europe looked like a model for the world. With rapid growth and cohesive societies, Europeans were among the happiest in the world. Why did the miracle abruptly come to an end?

There are two possible explanations. The first points to politics and the other to technology. We begin with politics. In the 1950s and

1960s Europeans worked very hard. Many European cities had been leveled during World War II. Factories were destroyed, and human capital was depleted by war casualties. This was not the time to think about leisure and consumption. Europeans had to dig in their heels and start to rebuild. By the end of the 1960s their resolve had success. Europeans could now raise their thoughts to the quality of their lives. Also the late 1960s was a period of political turmoil. From universities to factories, Europeans demanded less work with equal pay, labor regulations against firings, free education and free health care for everyone, and generous pensions to be enjoyed earlier in life. In the end, governments delivered what the people asked. European economies had been growing fast, and there seemed to be enough resources to accommodate all demands. Then came the oil crisis and at the same time, at least in some countries such as Germany and Italy, the fight for change became tough. To prevent students and workers from being lured by the call of the extreme left—these were the years of Bader Meinhof and the Red Brigades—governments kept accommodating even after it had become clear that the resources were no longer there. In the 1970s the welfare state was paid for through inflation and in the 1980s by building up public debt. From those years Europe inherited large governments and the high taxes needed to pay for it. In 1960, total government spending (the average for the pre-enlargement EU 15 countries) was 29 percent of GDP (the level of the United States today); in 1970, it was 37; in 1980, it was 47; and in 1990, it was 50 percent of GDP. The accompanying increase in taxes depressed growth. Some other factors, the oil shock in particular, contributed as well and compounded the fiscal deficiencies.

Had Europe continued to grow as in the 1950s and 1960s, the welfare demands of the 1970s could have been accommodated with more limited increases in tax rates. But in the 1970s the engine that until then had provided growth stopped working, and this is where the explanation based on technology comes into place. As economists Daron Acemoglu, Philippe Aghion, and Fabrizio Zilibotti argue in their academic work, European growth in the 1960s was—as Japan and Korea experienced later—largely of the catch-up type. Europeans started off, after World War II, far from the technological frontier: imitation of the best US technologies was enough for a fast pickup. As we will discuss later in the book, imitation works well with large incumbent and entrenched firms, a bank-centered financial system, long-term relationships, a slow turnover of managers, stable ownership of firms, and a hands-on approach by the government. Industrial policy did work in the 1960s in Europe, as it did later in Korea and Japan. But when Europe came closer to the technological frontier, and innovation rather than imitation became the critical factor for growth, Europe found itself ill prepared. The very institutions that had been responsible for the success of the 1960s became an obstacle to growth after the 1970s. Rather than speed up the destruction of old firms and favor the creation of new, innovative enterprises, Europeans kept on protecting incumbents and dreaming up industrial policy.

It is hard to see how Europe can turn around if it does not change profoundly, but we do not see enough energy for reforms. Germany has 5 million unemployed, the highest number since the Weimar Republic, but we see acquiescence rather than change. Italy and Portugal are falling behind even relative to Germany: exports are falling and productivity growth has virtually stopped. In both countries the political system is incapable of delivering reforms. What we see instead of reforms, are the attempts of insiders to protect themselves from the effects of economic integration and the globalization of markets. France is moving in a protectionist direction, that of the French fortress, the Asterix village. French farmers are heavily protected from the competition of farmers from developing countries. In Italy many believe that only tariffs can save their country from Chinese competition especially in the textile sector. These protectionist tendencies are worrisome.

The reader should be aware of oversimplifications. To begin with, we say Europe but we really mean continental Western Europe. In many dimensions Europeans have, vis-à-vis the United Kingdom, reactions that are similar to those elicited by the United States. The French veto on the proposed new European constitution was partly a vote against Tony Blair's alleged plans to reform the European social model along Anglo-Saxon lines. In Central and Eastern Europe some countries are adopting models quite different from those of continental Western Europe and closer to the Anglo-Saxon type. Even within Western Europe there are many differences. The Scandinavian countries, after suffering a deep crisis in the early 1990s, have been able to combine a far-reaching welfare state with market flexibility and decent growth. It is too early to say whether their current performance will be a long-lasting success. Hailing Nordic countries as an example of the superiority of the European economic model over that of the United States—an argument one often hears in Europe—is at least premature, but no doubt something very important is happening there. Unfortunately, the larger European countries—France, Germany, Italy, and Spain—do not show the political will and capability of adopting Nordic policies. Moreover the social cohesions and "social capital" so diffuse in Nordic countries and that greatly help their systems work well are lacking in southern Europe.

Interestingly, while Americans and Europeans have different views, they both seem happy with the societies in which they live. A recent poll asked people how they felt about their quality of life: eight European countries rank above the United States and seven below, with no clear pattern: Italy and Spain rank 8th and 10th, the United States 13th, France and Germany 25th and 26th. This suggests that Americans and Europeans pretty much get what they like: they are unlikely to want to switch sides of the Atlantic. By the way, even in Argentina most people claimed to be happy right up to the day of the crisis!

So is there no problem? Well, yes and no. It is certainly true that by and large European policies reflect the will of the electorate, as they should in democracies. Europeans are certainly not free marketers trapped by interventionist politicians. However, the Europeans' aversion to market liberalism is often strategically fostered by groups of insiders who benefit from market protection. This is indeed one of the major themes of this book.

In recent years numerous signs of dissatisfaction (still not well channeled politically) have been arising in France, Germany, and Italy. In all three cases one perceives frustration with an inability to implement reforms that are urgently needed. More important, lack of concern for serious reforms may simply reflect a failure to understand what is coming. The European decline is a slow process, and this makes reforms more difficult politically to accomplish. Crises often generate the impetus for reform, a slow decline less so. In Latin America, for instance, certain countries, and especially Chile, emerged from a near catastrophic crisis in the 1970s and a period of dictatorship with a new vigor. The reforms in Chile have turned its emerging economy into one of the most successful in Latin America. From the 1950s onward Europe had no big crises, no hyperinflation nor hyper recession. An old saying goes, if you put a frog in cold water and start warming the water slowly until it boils, the frog dies. If you throw a frog in hot water, it jumps out and lives. Europe is that frog in slowly warming water.

Look at the facts. Partly because of high taxes, generous pensions, high unemployment benefits, and unions' insistence for fewer hours of work and partly because of attitudes, Europeans work less and less. Italian "kids" leave college at age 27; then they spend a couple of years looking for a job, they work 30 years, and eventually they retire at 60 and live until they are 90. The French have obtained a 35-hour week and in May and August very few are at work in France. In Germany peak hour traffic on a Friday is 2 pm. You can't grow very fast if you work fewer and fewer hours per person, unless your productivity grows at extraordinary rates. For this to happen, you need research and development and competitive universities, not to mention truly competitive product markets that promote the quick adoption of new technologies. Europe is deficient in all these dimensions. Rather than building upon its most talented young people, it does very little to stop them from migrating to the United States, tempted by US universities and US high-tech firms. About one-third of Harvard's economics department is Europeans who have fled their countries' troubled universities. Western Europe, instead of trying to attract the most talented youths from India, China, and Eastern Europe, restricts migration. The immigrants allowed are not the smart people who in the United States have created the many innovative start-ups. The best educated Central and Eastern Europeans are flying over Western Europe and going to the United States. "Wait ten years to open your borders to my fellow citizens," recently said the then Romanian foreign minister, "and every smart Romanian engineer will have migrated to the United States: what you'll get will be our uneducated peasants."

Europeans are growing older. Fertility rates are exceptionally low. Europe won't thrive if only a few people work to support an increasing number of retirees. The closed borders and irrational immigration policies promise to make the European aging populations amid low birth rates harder to sustain. These two demographic trends will seriously strain European budgets.

Economic decline and political decline go hand in hand. Because of its large social spending and the low growth rate, Europe cannot support a powerful military. Sooner rather than later Europe will lose its powerful role in international organizations. Already today people around the world, especially in Asia, are wondering why France and Britain should have permanent seats in the UN Security Council. Countries like China and India with population sizes orders of magnitudes larger than France, Britain, and Germany combined will soon demand and obtain more power in world politics, and rightly so. At the moment these countries are determined to work hard and become rich. Pretty soon they will succeed and call for more recognition at the political tables of world organizations. European countries will have to move over.

The organization and allocation of power in international organizations, from the UN to the IMF and the G7 (now G8) meetings, still reflects a post–Second World War equilibrium that has become obsolete. At that time Germany and Japan were the defeated aggressors; the Soviets were a threat, Germany was divided and a wall was about to be built. Much of the then-called Third World was either recently independent or a colony but still very poor. Times have changed: there were 74 independent countries in the world in 1945, and there are 193 today. Communism outside of China, Cuba, and North Korea is popular only in Parisian cafés; Germany is reunited; the Third World is growing faster than the First World. Computer software is now mostly developed in Bangalore; graduate programs in the United States, including business schools, admit thousands of smart Asian students. Times have changed; France and Britain continue to have permanent seats on the UN Security Council and Italy, not China, is part of the G7. Not for long.

Europe's lack of military spending also affects growth directly, since much of cutting edge technology is developed in military contracts. In the United States many high-tech firms, if they are really good, thrive thanks to contracts with the Pentagon. In Europe instead of military contracts firms often receive state subsidies, which is a much less efficient way of stimulating research and innovation. Europe could prevent its rapid military and political decline by pulling together resources (political and military) with a true foreign policy through the European Union. But recent experience suggests that European countries are very far from reaching any resemblance of this, and in fact they are walking away from any further political integration.

So is the Untied States of Europe a way out of Europe's decline? Yes and no. As an economic area the European Union has worked relatively well. As a form of political union, however, the rapid annihilation of the proposed constitution has shown the severe limits of this process. The idea of a European political union that balances the United States in the international arena seems less and less realistic every day.

The hurdles that stand in the way of a United Europe also stem from one of Europe's main advantages: its diversity—diversity of language, of culture, of historical experience, and of lifestyle. Diversity may prevent Europe from exploiting the potential of unity, but a diverse society could be in a better position to adapt to change. In a rapidly changing world this could be Europe's most important asset. Europe should embrace diversity both within its ranks and with reference to non-Europeans. Instead, Brussels' insistence on coordination and uniformity is in sharp contrast with the "Let a thousand flowers bloom" view of the world. In the area of diversity Europeans could learn from the Unites States. Americans have had a history of dealing with racial and ethnic diversity, and it is as both an asset and a liability. It is an asset because being a successful melting pot is what has made America great. It is a liability because many of the social problems in the United States are associated with race relations. Europe has the opportunity to learn from this experience, or it can sit back and pontificate about American failings. The view of French youths of African descent rioting in

Paris in November 2005 shocked the same Parisian intellectuals who led the May 68 riots. Troubling as these riots seemed, they are, unfortunately, the wave of the future.

Europe is at a crossroad. It can continue with business as usual and accept a slow but permanent decline. Or it can initiate reforms. Change is difficult, of course, where attitudes and institutions have deep roots in history and in political and intellectual traditions. But change is needed if an economic decline is to be avoided. Today the choice is still readily available; another decade of decline may foreclose this option.

Often the Europeans who worry about Europe's problems respond by proposing a long list of very detailed policies. Often they call for more public spending on infrastructure, education, industrial policies, and support for depressed areas. Our view is different. Europe does not need more public money in a myriad of programs. Europe needs reforms that create incentives and make its people willing to work hard and longer, take risks, and innovate. Europe needs more competition, not more public infrastructures. European universities need more "market incentives," not more public money. European firms need lower taxes, less heavily regulated labor markets, and better functioning product markets, not more subsidies and protection. This does not mean that Europe simply needs to adopt the entire US model. Indeed there are aspects of the European welfare state that are efficient and should be preserved. But too often the benefits to overprotected insiders get precedence over the needs of the general public and, in particular, at a cost to the younger generation.

Some observers are talking about the twenty-first century being the European century, the same as the twentieth century was the American century. We take a more skeptical view: there is as good a chance that the twenty-first century will be the century of European decline. We hope to be proved wrong.

1

Europe and the United States: Two Different Social Models

Americans and Europeans think differently about poverty, inequality, redistribution of income from the rich to the poor, social protection, and welfare. Americans by and large believe that the poor should help themselves. Europeans, on the contrary, believe that the government is primarily responsible to lift people out of poverty. In a recent academic paper Rafael Di Tella, Robert Mc Culloch, and one of the authors of this book (Alesina) found that Europeans consider themselves less happy when inequality increases even as many other individual and social indicators that determine a person's happiness remain constant. Americans, on the other hand, do not consider themselves to be less happy as inequality increases, and neither are the American poor as upset by inequality as the European rich are.

This is one critical difference between the two sides of the Atlantic that has major policy implications for the role of government, taxation, regulation, public spending, education, migration, and social cohesion. Deep down, this different way of thinking matters for almost every single policy issue that we examine in this book.

To some extent, this is a difference of preferences on the two sides of the Atlantic; Europeans freely and willingly choose to have a larger welfare state, with all the associated costs in terms of taxation and regulation, because they dislike inequality. So, is there no

---

This chapter is based on A. Alesina and E. Glaeser, 2004, *Fighting Poverty in the US and Europe: A World of Difference*, Oxford University Press, Oxford.

problem? Not quite. Government intervention and regulation, when set in motion on a large scale, often have undesired effects such as of creating pockets of privilege, overprotected categories (for example, public employees), a culture of "dependency" on public polices, reduction in the predisposition to take risks. There is a lot of "tax churning" too: government taxes with one hand, introducing distortions, and with the other hand returns goods, services, and transfers to the same people it has taxed. In some cases certain so-called redistributive schemes end up increasing rather than reducing inequality, especially when insiders "capture" those programs.

All of the above generates resistance to change. A typical political strategy for overprotected categories of insiders is to claim that any change to their status will increase inequality and poverty. So one of the key questions for Europe, and one of the major themes of this book, is how to reduce excessive inequality without falling into these traps. Since this different way of thinking about inequality is so critical, we need to examine where it comes from. In particular, it matters for an understanding of how to design reforms that can be politically feasible and economically successful.

Before launching into this contentious terrain, we give a caveat and some numbers. First the caveat: a "European" welfare state does not exist. There is wide variation among welfare systems in Europe. The countries that comprise continental Western Europe (Europe in short) organize their welfare systems differently. We will discuss later on in this book some of these differences, but they have in common one fundamental characteristic: an extensive involvement of the state in redistribution and social protection to a much larger extent than in the United States.

A few numbers: Europe spends twice as much as the United States on social programs (roughly 20 percent versus 10 percent), and total government spending in Europe is close to 50 percent of GDP, whereas in the United States, government consumes about 30 percent of GDP (table 1.1). Europe also spends much more than developing countries, but the United States is a better comparison because typically the size of government goes up with per capita income. Nowhere else on earth are governments as large as in continental Western Europe.

Europe spends more than the United States on every social program, but especially on the unemployed and on poor families, which are some of the programs more directly targeted to poverty per se and not related to old age, disease, and so on. Public pensions are more generous in Europe than in the United States (table 1.2). While, in principle, public pensions take from the young to give to the old, and are not meant to be redistributive, in practice, they are. They redistribute from the rich young to the poor old. In

Table 1.1
General government expenditures as percentage of GDP, 2000

Country	Total[a]	Goods and services	Wages and salaries	Subsidies	Social benefits and other transfers[b]	Gross investment
United States	29.9	5.3	9.2	0.4	10.6	3.3
Continental Europe[c]	44.9	8.3	12.4	1.5	17.6	2.5
France	48.7	9.7	13.5	1.3	19.6	3.2
Germany	43.3	10.9	8.1	1.7	20.5	1.8
Sweden	52.2	9.8	16.4	1.5	20.2	2.2
United Kingdom	37.3	11.4	7.5	0.4	15.6	1.1

Source: A. Alesina and E. Glaeser (2004: *Fighting Poverty in the US and Europe a World of Difference*, Oxford University Press, table 2.1). Original source: Authors' calculations based on data from *OECD Economic Outlook Database* (no. 71, vol. 2002, release 01, June 2002).
a. Totals include interest payments and some categories of capital outlays.
b. Includes social security.
c. Simple average for Austria, Belgium, Denmark, Finland, France, Germany, Greece, Italy, Netherlands, Norway, Portugal, Spain, and Sweden.

Table 1.2
Government expenditures on social programs as percentage of GDP, 1998

Country	Total	Old-age, disability and survivors	Family[a]	Unemployment and labor market programs	Health[b]	Other[c]
United States	14.6	7.0	0.5	0.4	5.9	0.9
Continental Europe[d]	25.5	12.7	2.3	2.7	6.1	1.7
France	28.8	13.7	2.7	3.1	7.3	2.1
Germany	27.3	12.8	2.7	2.6	7.8	1.5
Sweden	31.0	14.0	3.3	3.9	6.6	3.2
United Kingdom	24.7	14.2	2.2	0.6	5.6	2.0

Source: Alesina and Glaeser (2004). Original source: Authors' calculations based on data from *OECD Social Expenditure Database* 1980–1998 (3rd ed., 2001).
a. Includes cash benefits and in kind services.
b. Includes inpatient care, ambulatory medical services, and pharmaceutical goods.
c. Includes occupational injury and disease benefits, sickness benefits, housing benefits, and expenditure on other contingencies (both in cash or in kind), as well as benefits to low-income households.
d. Simple averages for Austria, Belgium, Denmark, Finland, France, Germany, Greece, Italy, Netherlands, Norway, Portugal, Spain, and Sweden.

fact poor retirees receive more than the rich retirees, relative to their pre-pension incomes and relative to their contributions.

There is wide variation in how redistributive pension systems are organized within Europe. Pensions are much less redistributive in Germany than in Sweden, for instance, but on average pensions are more redistributive in Europe than in the United States. Differences between Europe and the United States are also apparent on the tax side. In the United States the income tax is much less progressive than in Europe on average, even though there is much variation within Europe.

However, fiscal policy is not the only way by which European governments *try to redistribute* income. Other policies include labor market regulations, minimum wage rules, and public education, just to name a few. We have chosen the wording "try to redistribute" for a reason. Not all these programs are efficient in directing flows of resources toward the truly poor; most are advantageous for the middle class and a host of protected categories (special interests). For example, labor regulations protect insiders in the labor market and union members while creating obstacles for the unemployed and the young seeking to (re)enter the labor market. Pension systems could be partly privatized without increasing inequality. Public spending on tertiary education is at most neutral from a distributional point of view, since mostly the rich attend universities, and indeed they pay a larger share of taxes. Again, there is much variation within Europe. Generally, economists characterize the Nordic welfare states as a success; the Mediterranean ones (Italy, France, and Spain) as more problematic.

So why are Europeans so concerned about inequality compared to Americans? A possible explanation is that there is more need to redistribute in Europe because there is more before-tax inequality. But that is not the case: before-tax inequality is much larger in the United States than in Europe for a number of reasons but mainly because of a higher return from investment in education in the United States and the consequent steeper salary structure. Therefore more redistribution in the United States should compensate for the higher before-tax inequality. Instead it is just the opposite.

So why are social protection systems so different on the two sides of the Atlantic? A few numbers speak volumes. According to the World Value Survey, a respected attitudinal study conducted in about 40 countries, 60 percent of Americans believe that the poor are lazy, a view shared by only 26 percent of Europeans. The almost exact opposite proportions (60 percent of Europeans and 29 percent of Americans) believe that the poor are trapped in poverty. The American poor do not mind inequality because they see it as a rung on the social ladder they can climb. The European poor, however, see inequality as an insurmountable obstacle. Once, one of the authors of this book was mentioning to a friend these statistics in an elevator in Washington, DC, and an African-American janitor in the same elevator immediately agreed that the poor should help themselves, that it was not the role of government to step in. Try to find a janitor with similar views in Paris!

Why are views so different on the two sides of the Atlantic? One possible explanation is that America is a more mobile society, where the poor believe they can escape poverty if they try hard enough. If the poor remain poor, it must be because they are lazy. The European poor on the other hand, lack the supposed opportunities that poor Americans have, since European societies are less mobile.

The question is then whether there is more social mobility in the United States than in Europe, and this is an immensely difficult question to answer. Sure America did not have European-style noblesse, and no feudal system that generated a separation of social classes. Karl Marx had observed this difference between the United States and Europe as the source of the less well-defined US class system relative to Europe, and as having made class-based parties and movements in the United States more difficult to prosper. He was, of course, right. In America individual histories of accumulated riches from humble beginnings (the self-made man) are countless and continue to this day. The self-made man is the American icon. The evidence is the scores of Europeans in the nineteenth and early twentieth century who left the old continent in search for riches across the Atlantic and aggrandized themselves in an American-style aristocracy.

So do the American poor today have better prospects of escaping poverty than the European poor? One way of measuring actual mobility is as the fraction of various income groups moving up and down the social ladder. Academic research shows that according to this measure one does not see much of a difference between the two sides of the Atlantic. However, an enthusiastic supporter of the American social model can still argue that the possibilities of escaping poverty exist but the American poor do not take advantage of them. Europeans can still argue, instead, that whatever effort the poor exert, they are simply trapped and cannot escape poverty without the help of public social programs.

One thing is certain: while available statistical evidence on measured social mobility shows that the latter is not very different between the United States and Europe, Americans view society as very "mobile" while Europeans see it as "immobile." So either the Americans overestimate the amount of mobility or Europeans underestimate it. Given their belief in the immobility of society, Europeans also think that the poor need much help in a variety of ways and the government has to intervene heavily to provide opportunities, income, social protection, even at the cost of a heavy burden of taxation, market regulation, and various interferences with market forces.

Although reforms to the welfare state are under discussion in Europe, all the reforms proposed would still keep European redistributive policies much more extensive than those in the United States. Europeans are proud of their European models of welfare. The attitude of Americans instead, that individuals can escape poverty by taking advantage of market opportunities, has also to do with the cost of taxation. It bothers the average American much more to pay higher taxes, so government intervention is viewed suspiciously. But, whereas raising taxes is a "capital sin" in American politics, cutting spending is a "capital sin" in European politics. Every time someone mentions spending cuts in Europe, it has to be followed by a long list of platitudes stating the benefits of "productive" government, spending in education, research, social protection, and the like. What exactly remains to cut after all these exceptions is rather unclear.

These differences about the perceived benefits of government spending are not a recent phenomenon. They run deep into the histories of the two continents. Figure 1.1 shows that differences in the evolution of social spending in the United States and Europe go back to the very beginnings of state interventions in these market economies.

Until the late nineteenth century government spending, except for the military, was very small. As nonmilitary government expenditures started to increase, they immediately grew faster in Europe than in the United States. In the twentieth century there were bursts of increases in the United States, in particular, on the New Deal and later the Great Society, but Europe on average outpaced the United States. Therefore explanations of the difference between Europe and the United States cannot be found in recent political events; they run deep into the history of these two places.

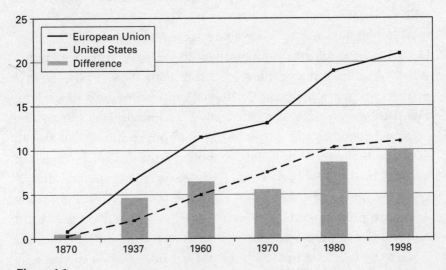

Figure 1.1
Government subsidies and transfers as percentage of GDP, 1870 to 1998. Source: Alesina and Glaeser (2004)

Where did these European and American differences of view in the twentieth century come from? To begin with, European culture was and remains profoundly affected by the Marxist intellectual tradition (broadly defined). The Marxist concept of "class" implies that it is almost impossible for a poor person to become rich, or, apropos of the tradition, for a proletarian to become a capitalist. Marxism has to assume social immobility to justify the concept of class; otherwise, its basic construct collapses.

The Marxist influence has not been limited to intellectuals and students. In many European countries political institutions were shaped in revolutionary periods during which socialist parties and ideas enjoyed widespread support. For example, socialist and communist parties, especially in the early 1920s, demanded and obtained electoral systems based on proportional representation. Those systems allowed the entry in national parliaments of the Marxist parties which then started to influence the making of welfare policies. Even when they were in the opposition, those parties, often supported by street movements and strikes, were very influential. As it happened, proportional representation was a factor in the implementation of redistributive policies because it provided a political voice to minorities. Indeed several statistical studies have shown that today in every industrial democracy the size of public redistributive spending increases with the degree of proportionality in the electoral system.

The American Constitution, although amended and modified, is still the document drafted almost 250 years ago by a group of white wealthy men. The European constitutions that are today in place were written in the nineteenth century, often at times of turmoil and by national assemblies with representation of Marxist parties. They certainly are different from the American Constitution in their emphasis on social rights and in the degree of protection of property rights. Today very few parties in Europe call themselves Marxist or communist. The Marxist influence we

because they perceive such policies as favoring racial minorities. Even poor whites often oppose redistributive policies, owing to racial distrust.

But why should a white person be predisposed to object to welfare spending if he or she perceives that it benefits racial minorities? Much experimental and statistical evidence shows that individuals trust and associate more with others of the same race; possibly this is a natural, though unpleasant, instinct. Indeed the effect of ethnic diversity on redistributive policies is by no means a US-only phenomenon. Figure 1.2 highlights an inverse relationship between social spending and a measure of ethnic fractionalization in a cross section of countries.

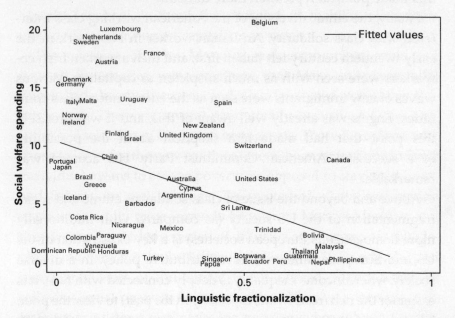

Figure 1.2
Linguistic fractionalization and social welfare spending. Linguistic fractionalization is a measure of "a country's homogeneity." In technical terms, the fractionalization index is the probability that two randomly drawn individuals from a country speak the same language. The more the country is linguistically homogeneous, the lower is the index. Source: Alesina and Glaeser (2004)

At least up to now European countries have been more racially homogeneous than the United States, and this may explain the difference in welfare policies. Whether or not European countries can continue to be homogeneous by restricting immigration remains to be seen, as we discuss in the next chapter.

Racial considerations also influence the nature of America's political institutions, thus reinforcing a predisposition against redistributive policies. Proportional representation, widely adopted in Europe in the first decades of the twentieth century, was never embraced by the United States because it was viewed as a system that would allow black representatives (and socialists) to be elected. "First pass the post" systems, especially with gerrymandering (the rearrangement of the boundaries of congressional districts to influence the outcome of elections), would ensure instead an underrepresentation of minorities.

Many redistributive programs in the United States are run by the fifty states. States that are more racially heterogeneous have smaller redistributive programs relative to their levels of income. Welfare is plentiful in the overwhelmingly white states of the north and northwest (Oregon and Minnesota, to cite two examples) and in some states in New England (for example, Vermont). It is lacking in the racially mixed southeast and southwest. Figure 1.3 shows the inverse relationship between an important state-run welfare program that provides support for poor families with children (AFDC: Aid to Families with Dependent Children) and the share of black population in the state. So the decentralized character of the United States creates yet another obstacle for redistributive policies.

Finally the labor unions function differently. In the United States unions have always behaved as organizations that bargain directly with employers for wage and other concessions. Because of a lack of friendly parties in government for much of US history, American unions have viewed government intervention suspiciously. They want to keep government out of their business. In contrast,

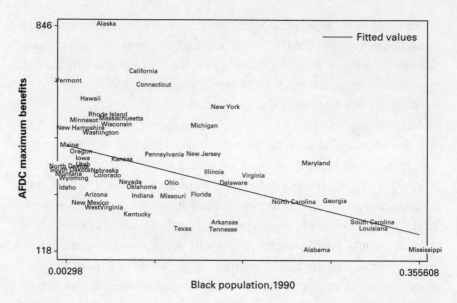

Figure 1.3
Maximum AFDC benefits and percentages of blacks across the US states. (AFDC is
a welfare program administered by US states that provides aid to low-income
families with dependent children.) Source: Alesina and Glaeser (2004)

European unions, in alliances with Social Democratic parties, which
are often in office, have developed a bargaining system that
involves three-party negotiations with business associations and
the government as a mediator (and as an employer in the case of
public employees). The result has been that welfare policies become
a matter of bargaining in tripartite negotiations.

Are there pressures on the European welfare system to become
more like the American system? To a certain extent, yes. One is
demographic pressure. European pension systems are in great
danger of insolvency because of the demographic trends of lower
birth rates and lengthening life expectancies. A second, less obvious,
element in the next decade may heavily influence the future of
the European welfare state, and it has to do with immigration and
racial diversity in Europe. Continental Europe is already becoming,

and will become more so, ethnically mixed as more newcomers from Eastern Europe and the developing world arrive. Based on our earlier discussion, this may put some pressure on the state to trim welfare. It will not be long before even Europe's more respectable conservative parties weigh in on rhetoric about foreigners coming to feast off of their citizens' taxes. Simply put, as middle-class Europeans begin to recognize that a good portion of their poor are recent immigrants, their ingrained belief in the virtue of the welfare state will begin to crumble. Today even Europe's leftist intelligentsia openly associate crime and urban squalor with immigration. The step from there to lamenting the high taxes spent on welfare for immigrants is a short one.

So what have we learned in this chapter? Europeans have been much more influenced than Americans by the Marxist tradition. They view market-induced inequality as a major evil. They are generally suspicious of markets and favor massive government intervention to correct for inequality. The fact that European societies are (or at least have been) relatively homogeneous has favored the adoption of very generous social protection policies often promoted by unions and Social Democratic Party alliances, sometimes directly against business interests. Redistribution per se, once its costs and the implied trade-off are well understood and accepted by a society, can be a desirable social goal. But European welfare states have generated three kinds of problems, which we take on in much detail later on in this book. The first is that an excessive generosity of welfare systems adopted in periods of high growth has created fiscal problems for the budgets of many European countries, especially where growth has slowed down and demographic trends have turned negative. The second is that massive government intervention and regulation have contributed to create pockets of insider privilege and many overprotected groups that, in turn, oppose change. Finally, there is third less obvious but potentially even more insidious effect, suggested in a recent academic paper by George Marios Angeletos of MIT and one of the authors of this book (Alesina). High taxes and regulations create a disincentive effect that makes society less mobile because individual initiative is stifled. It follows that some of those who become rich either are lucky or have managed to navigate the complexity of the regulatory systems. In other words, where high taxes and complex regulatory systems are abundant, there often thrive gray areas of complicated business and tax laws, not to mention tax evasions. The perception that those who made it simply "played the system" then raises a vicious circle of demand for redistribution, taxation, and regulation. The more governments tax and regulate, the less society is mobile and the less individual effort and investments are rewarded, and so the higher is the demand for redistribution and for taxes. This is the vicious circle that countries in Europe should seek to break.

Why don't European taxpayers object? Taxpayer complacency has also to do indirectly with the Marxist attitude we discussed earlier. Europeans tend to see each other as members of a group: teachers, public employees, cab drivers, union members, and so on. They identify themselves much more than Americans with an economic and social group, somewhat like Marxist consciousness of "class." To a much lesser extent than Americans, they see themselves as individual taxpayers. Politicians respond more to pressure from "groups" rather than pressure from taxpayers. The result is the increase in spending programs and an impediment to stand against "groups," even the less deserving ones.

So what is the answer for Europe? Simply adopt the American welfare system? The answer is no. As we argued, there is genuine difference in preferences over social policies on the two sides of the Atlantic. The problem for Europe is how to design welfare systems that are fiscally solvent and not create all the political and economic distortions that we have just discussed. The task ahead is not easy.

2   Handling a Multiethnic Society

The tiny strait of Gibraltar could be easily covered by a bridge. It separates Europeans from 210 million Northern Africans whose average per capita income is US$1,800 a year and 700 million sub-Saharan Africans whose average per capita income is $500 a year; in contrast, the average income of Western Europeans is US$22,800. The collapse of communism in Central and Eastern Europe has allowed 350 million Central and Eastern Europeans to move freely. Of these potential migrants, 70 million would come from countries that are now members of the European Union. Continuing turbulence in the Middle East has created emigration from that region in the northwest direction.

The size of migration into Western Europe can become gigantic, and immigration will be one of the important questions for Europe in the next decade, if not the most important issue. Many people seeking immigration, certainly those from Northern Africa and the Middle East, are Muslim, share a culture that appears increasingly difficult to integrate with Western values. In this sense the immigration challenge Europe faces is more daunting than similar problems in the United States, where the immigrants are mostly from the Catholic countries of Latin America. Europeans are far behind in their thinking; if a wake-up call to Europeans is necessary, on the immigration issue, the call has to be especially loud.

Once again, a cross-Atlantic comparison is useful. The United States, as a country of immigrants, is much better prepared to deal with the issues raised by waves of immigration. One the most studied areas in economics and sociology today is the effect of racial heterogeneity on the functioning of the US society. Europe has a lot to learn from the United States in terms of what to do and what not to do.

The broad lesson that the US case provides is fascinating and complex. The American melting pot has been a gigantic economic success. However, managing the social problems related to ethnic and racial diversity has not been easy. Diversity is at the same time one of the greatest assets and one of the greatest headaches of the United States. Many of America's cities have been stressed by difficult race relations. New York and Los Angeles, the two most ethnically diverse cities in the United States, are also America's leaders in business and in the arts. But both cities (Los Angeles, in particular) have experienced race-related riots. Race relations in the United States have been for decades—and remain—at the center of political debate, to the point where racial cleavages are as important as income, if not more, as determinants of political preferences and attitudes.

The first step necessary to address the race relations problem realistically is to understand the origin and consequences of racial animosity, even if it means uncovering unpleasant truths. In the case of the United States, research in economics, sociology, psychology, and political science has shown that people of different races trust each other much less; whites are less willing to support welfare spending because it is perceived to favor minorities, as we discussed in the previous chapter. More racially fragmented communities have less efficient governments, more corruption and patronage, more crime, and fewer productive public goods per tax dollar. In one word, racially diverse cities have more social problems and less social capital, although some of them are among the most productive (New York and Los Angeles, for example).

The difficulty in running racially mixed cities does not mean that the answer is to eliminate heterogeneity and create racially homogeneous communities. But an acknowledgment of the reality of these issues is needed in order to start constructing solid public policies toward race relations. Americans disagree on how to do this. Some favor affirmative action programs that provide preferences for minorities in college admissions, job allocations, and public contracts. These policies are seen as a way of offering reparation for past injustices and, more important, for creating role models and for overcoming residual and more or less voluntary discrimination. Others object to affirmative action, and argue that a race-blind policy coupled with free markets and pro-family values are all that are necessary to create jobs for minorities and help keep black families together. The latter is a crucial factor in any policy, since one of the single most important causes of poverty in the United States is the diffusion of single parents (read, single mother) households in the black community.

There are other debates: Are black colleges (universities only for blacks) a good or a bad idea? What is the social peer pressure in black neighborhoods? Why are black young women doing better than their male counterparts? What is the relationship among different racial minorities, say, black and Chinese? This is not the place to offer original solutions to the question of racial harmony in the United States, but it is clear that multiracial and multiethnic cities in the United States pose a challenge but are one of the sources of the country's vitality. The critical question is how to keep the good and correct the bad of racial heterogeneity.

Regardless of what the correct answers are, America is continually trying to find them, by trial and error, and determining what to do about breaches in race relations has dominated US politics.

Overall, minorities have made great progress toward more integration and economic success. In the 1950s, southern blacks could not sit in the front of buses; it took a courageous black woman, Rosa Parks, to challenge this rule. Today, a black woman is the US Secretary of State. But the economic position of minorities in the United States is far from perfect. Poverty remains unduly concentrated among minorities. As we discussed in the previous chapter, often racial concerns prevent the adoption of rational welfare policies. Minorities choosing to segregate themselves in their own communities compound these problems.

Reading the European newspapers one often perceives snobbishness toward the United States when it comes to racial issues. They, the Americans, have problems with racism; we are immune from it, except for crazed neo-Nazi skinheads, and their like. The disturbing images of the victims of hurricane Katrina, which showed the destitution of poor minorities, gave a big boost to the European superiority complex. But what happened in 2005, from Amsterdam to Paris, shows that the race problem in Europe is deepseated as well. As in the United States, the sad truth is that race relations are inherently difficult, and trust and cooperative behavior do not travel well across racial lines. If Europeans think that their society can easily handle a growing number of foreign immigrants of different races and cultures they are spinning fairy tales. The riots in France in November 2005 were a brutal awakening for Europeans, and this is just the beginning of a long arduous process of acclimation.

Racism and use of immigration as a political wedge are becoming the agenda of Europe's right. The Lega Nord in Italy, the former Vlaams Blok (now named Vlaams Belang after the original party was declared a criminal organization and disbanded) in Belgium, and Le Pen's National Front in France are examples of parties that share an aversion toward immigrants and promote simplistic policies to control them. While individuals like Jorg Haidar and

Jean-Marie Le Pen may come and (never too soon) go, the race question will not disappear from European politics anytime soon. Even some of the words used by French Interior Minister Sarkozy during the Paris riots showed at the very best naiveté in how to handle delicate racial issues, and at worst arrogance.

How is the European intelligentsia reacting to immigration? Thus far at its dinner parties it is has been acceptable to argue that recent immigration has increased crime, while it would be in bad taste to argue against welfare for immigrants or in favor of other discriminatory rules. But these issues will be on the table soon. If immigrants commit crimes, should we also reward them with welfare? This is especially pressing because various studies show that immigrants tend to be heavy users of welfare benefits. This question, as of today unacceptable at the good European society tables, will soon come under scrutiny.

Sweden is a case in point. Immigration started on a large scale in the late 1970s and early 1980s as a result of the open policy vis-à-vis refugees and asylum seekers. Following a period of humanitarian enthusiasm, problems began to appear. Eventually episodes of racism forced Sweden to face the problem of how to deal with a large immigrant population.

So how should Europeans think about immigration policy? The first step is to eliminate from the table "extreme" policies that make no sense: open borders completely and let everyone enter who wants in, or seal the borders completely and keep everyone out.

The problem with the first solution is obvious: Europe cannot afford all of a sudden to welcome large portions of poor Africans. That would create tremendous social problems in Europe. But then, if migration from Africa is restricted, Europe should allow free trade in goods that can be a substitute for trade in factors of production (labor). As we will discuss below, the protectionist agricultural policy of Europe has severely damaged the economies of many

African countries that export agricultural products. If the European agricultural policy were more sensible and fair, African economies could make more progress and the desire of Africans to move to Europe would diminish.

The opposite extreme has problems too. Europe needs immigrants. Its population is aging, as we discussed in the Introduction, and the dependency ratio in Europe has increased tremendously. The population of individuals aged 60 and older as a percentage of the population aged 15 to 59 was 26 in 1990, it was 35 in 2000, and now it is higher. The number of births per thousand inhabitants fell from 1970 to 2000 from 16.8 to 9.3 in Italy, 13.4 to 9.4 in West Germany, 19.6 to 9.8 in Spain, 16.7 to 13.2 in France. The aging of the population in Italy, with the second lowest birth rate in Europe, is especially troublesome: Italy has the lowest share of population below the age of 20 in Europe (see figure 2.1).

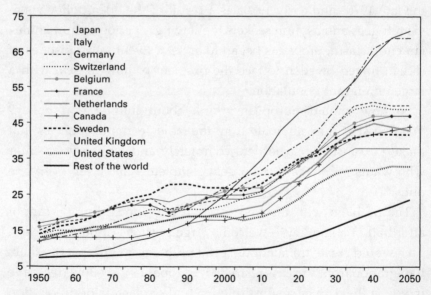

Figure 2.1
Old age dependency: Ratio of population aged 65 years and over as a percentage of population aged 15 to 64 years. Source: UN Population Division, *World Population Prospects, 2004*

The number of immigrants is particularly low in Spain and Italy (see table 2.1). Sweden stands out as the EU country with the largest number of immigrants, as a share of the population. Not surprisingly, Sweden is also the EU country where the thinking on immigration policy is more advanced. Austria also has a relatively high number of immigrants, but mostly composed of recent immigrants from Eastern Europe.

But, besides the demographic effects, immigration has other consequences. The inflow of skilled labor increases competition, stimulates innovation, and opens up new opportunities for the development of human capital. Today the United States is the preferred destination of many bright young men and women in search of markets to apply their skills. For the high-skilled worker even in a post–September 11 era it is easy to obtain a resident permit in the United States and then citizenship. Immigration can also serve the purpose of reducing rents of certain groups. The recent surfeit of Polish plumbers that scared so many French might have been

Table 2.1
Stock of migrants as percentage of population, 2000

Country	Stock of migrants
Belgium	8.6
Austria	9.4
Italy	2.8
Netherlands	9.9
Portugal	2.3
France	10.7
Finland	2.6
Germany	8.9
Spain	3.1
Sweden	11.2
Denmark	5.7
Ireland	8.1
United Kingdom	6.8
Greece	4.9

Source: Word Bank, World Development Indicators.

inopportune for the expensive plumbers in Paris, but how about the Parisians that need to hire cheaper plumbers?

Sealing the borders of Europe is both wrong and impossible. So how has Europe dealt with the problem? The first to knock at Europe's door were the citizens of the new member states from Central and Eastern Europe. These were highly educated people who could easily assimilate. It looked as if the old EU states would let most of them in right away. Instead this will not happen for many years. Worried about an invasion of migrant workers from Central and Eastern Europe, the original EU members have erected high barriers in order to prevent the flow. Despite the open market rhetoric of the Europe Union, for most citizens of the new member states free labor mobility will not become a reality before 2010. This is a questionable policy.

To begin with, even if today EU borders were fully opened to the east, Western Europe would not be flooded by workers coming from Central and Eastern Europe. According to *An Agenda for a Growing Europe*, a report published by Oxford University Press in 2004 for the European Commission, if borders were fully open, no more than 250,000 to 450,000 workers would go west during the first two years, followed by around 100,000 to 200,000 annually thereafter. Over the first decade, the cumulative number of migrants might amount to between 1.5 and 4 million, that is, 2.4 to 5 percent of the total population in the new member states—and a tiny fraction of the total population in the fifteen original members of the European Union. This is consistent with a vast amount of statistical evidence that Europeans, both Westerners and Easterners, are relatively sedentary people. Language barriers and attachments to cultural and family roots make people stay put even when they can expect significant economic benefits from a move.

Second, the longer Europe waits before opening up its borders, the lower the quality of the human capital it will receive. As Mircea Geoana, Romania's young former Minister of Foreign Affairs, recently put it: "If the EU waits another seven or ten years before it opens up, the workers it will receive from my country will be the least qualified, peasants and individuals with low human capital: by then, the doctors, the architects and the engineers will all have migrated to the United States." Indeed this is precisely what happened with the Russians: the most qualified have gone to the United States. Europe has been unable to attract much more than a few oligarchs, who migrated to the French Riviera, and a handful of lively street singers.

Third, so long as the Union's borders remain closed, there is also a risk that foreign investment will fly over Western Europe and land in Central and Eastern Europe, where people are willing to work long hours, market regulations are less intrusive, and human capital is relatively high, since communist schools were good at technical training. These countries have opened their markets to foreign investors—and foreign investors are responding without delay.

Finally, in view of the high hopes that preceded entry into the European Union, a stinginess toward new members would trigger a backlash toward Western Europeans. Discrimination against the citizens of the new member countries can create big political problems for the European Union. The anti-Easterners rhetoric that marred the "no" vote on the European constitution in France was quite telling. Protecting jobs of French workers threatened by migrant workers was the most visible claim of the anti-constitution camp.

So opening the border to many skilled Central and Eastern Europeans is the correct policy and Western Europe should move faster on this. Open borders increase competition, increase human capital, and create very limited *negative* social repercussions. If French plumbers have to reduce their fees or work harder, so be it. Unfortunately, however, the few immigrants from the east will solve neither Western Europe's aging population problem nor the demands of the job markets.

There is then a second type of immigration that is potentially more problematic. As manufacturing is relocated to South East Asia, Europe is increasingly becoming a service economy. This means that the old manufacturing jobs need to be replaced by two types of service activities: the high-skilled (finance, education) and the low-skilled, the people who "wait" on the well paid high-skilled. Unfortunately, this is a fact: well-functioning welfare systems should be there to correct excessive inequality and poverty. Incidentally the services provided by many of these jobs cannot be "bought." Trade in goods and services is not, in this case, a substitute for labor mobility. When you make an airline reservation for a flight between Boston and Chicago the airline agent may answer in India, but the Indian waiter in a New York restaurant has to be physically in New York. So what about the millions of European unemployed? Many of them, especially those who lost their blue-collar jobs in the declining heavy industries, are unwilling or unable to take jobs in the service sector; many are even too old to retrain for higher level service jobs. The sad truth is that many of the unemployed are unemployable, and they will probably reach their age of retirement using various forms of welfare.

One reason why Europe finds it so difficult to adapt to the disappearance of the traditional blue-collar jobs is the rigidity of relative wages. In the United States, between the 1970s and 2000, the gap between the average wage and the wages of lower paid workers increased by 13 percent for men and 18 percent for women. In France and Germany the opposite happened: the gap was reduced for both men and women, by 4 percent and 10 percent respectively. This explains why there are so few low-skilled jobs in these countries, and why firms have replaced low-skilled workers with machines.

The available studies on the displacement effects of migration from outside the European Union, namely the loss of jobs for Western Europeans caused by immigration, suggest that the displacement will be small if not zero. In fact, if Europe is to keep functioning, immigration has to extend far beyond the highly educated, easy to assimilate citizens of Central and Eastern Europe to the Maghreb, India, and South East Asia not to mention North Africa. In many ways this is already happening: the Philippino caregiver for the elderly, the Peruvian housecleaner, and so forth. On Sunday afternoons in Milan, in Paris, and in every chic vacation town in Europe large groups of Asian women can be seen enjoying their time off from household work.

Although there is no easy solution to the immigration problems, the economically rational approach is selected immigration. Each country decides whom to let in, according to the needs of the labor market, and with an eye on the possible social costs in terms of race relations. In a sense this is the policy followed by countries like the United States, Australia, and Canada. For instance, the green card system in the United States allows the government to allocate work entry permits on the basis of the needs of the labor market. Europe should move in the same direction by issuing a certain number of work permits (such as could include eventual citizenship) as a function of the needs of the receiving country.

The caveat, however, is that European governments often make their decisions based not on rational analysis of country needs but under pressure of insider lobbies. For instance, it was French plumbers and nurses who lobbied against immigration of their Eastern European counterparts. As with many other policy issues discussed in this book, Europe risks going down the wrong policy paths to the extent that governments are captured by insiders. The pressures from domestic lobbies tend to make migration policies excessively restrictive. The clear alternative is to create incentives for the government to err on the side of allowing more people in.

More difficult issues remain regarding race relations. If Europe's mainstream parties do not begin serious investment in understanding racial tensions and make race one of their priorities, individuals like Le Pen are bound to fill the void with their messages of hate.

3   Americans at Work, Europeans on Holiday

In the early 1970s, Europeans and Americans worked about the same number of hours; today, Europeans work much less, as figure 3.1 illustrates. In 1973, in the United States, France, Germany, and Italy the hours worked per year per person of working age (15–64) were about 1,800; today, they are about the same number in the United States, and they are around 1,400 in these three European countries. The UK worker is somewhere in between.

Why did this happen? And what are the consequences for economic growth, which lately has been lagging in Europe relative to the United States?

In a nutshell there are two views on this. One is that Europeans simply enjoy leisure more than Americans. But up to the mid-1970s Europeans worked more than Americans. So to be more precise, relative to Americans, as Europeans became rich, they switched more of their time into consumption of leisure rather than production of income to buy goods. And, the story continues, as hinted by some who hold this view, Europe is in some ways superior to the United States because Europeans have more fun and still keep up a good living standard and decent growth rates.

This chapter draws upon A. Alesina, E. Glaeser, and B. Sacerdote, 2004, Work and leisure in the US and Europe: Why so different? *NBER Macroeconomic Annual*, MIT Press.

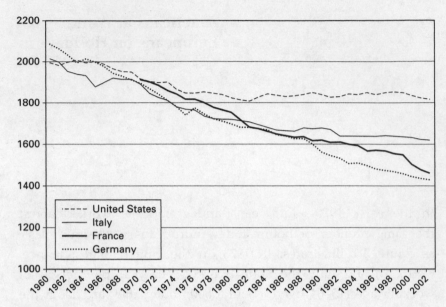

Figure 3.1
Hours worked annually over last four decades. Source: Alesina, Glaeser, and
Sacerdote (2004)

Apparently, so they claim, Europeans are aware of the trade-off
between working less and producing less and have made a well-
thought-out choice.

The other view is that Europeans work less and less because of
taxation on labor income and because of regulations imposed by
unions on hours worked, vacation time, overtime, and retirement
age. According to this view, work hours have fallen so low in
Europe because of the confluence of all these distortions, which are
also creating a major impediment to income growth and solvency
problems for pension systems. As the story continues, Europeans
do not grasp the danger of this trend and continue to live in the
dream that they can take more and more vacations, retire early, and
have one spouse stay at home, while enjoying an ever-increasing
level of income.

Which view is right? We believe that the second, more pessimistic scenario comes closer to reality. This does not mean that the first story should be completely disregarded. Even if Europe where to eliminate all distortions, working hours will never rise to the US level, probably because there are cultural differences in preferences. But we firmly believe that the distortions noted above (taxation, regulation, and pensions systems) that favor very early retirement have pushed some European countries, especially France, Germany, and Italy, way too far in the direction of working too little. By too little, we mean an amount that is too small to be compatible with the aspirations of modern-day Europeans about their expected incomes while working and while retired.

In addressing these questions more fully, we need to begin by looking at how Europeans work less than Americans. There are three reasons why hours worked by a person can be different. One is that a lower fraction of the population is employed when participation in the labor force is lower or when unemployment is higher. The second is that those who work take longer vacations or report sick more often or enjoy longer maternity leaves. The third is that normal hours in a week without vacation, and when the worker is not sick, are lower. All three factors can explain the US–Europe differences.

Table 3.1 provides a breakdown of the differences in hours worked per person in the United States compared with France, Germany, and Italy. Note that in France and Germany all three factors have a similar weight, roughly a third of the difference. In Italy the largest effect, by far, comes from lower participation in the work force. Further in Italy labor participation is especially low among men and women in their twenties and over fifty.

What do people do when they do not work in the market economy? They could be enjoying leisure activities, producing

Table 3.1
Differences of work hours in France, Germany, and United Kingdom compared
with work hours in United States

		Fraction of hours difference explained
Total hours per week per person		
United States	25.13	
France	17.95	
Germany	18.68	
Italy	16.68	
United States–France	7.18	1.00
United States–Germany	6.45	1.00
United States–Italy	8.45	1.00
Employment/population, 15–64		
United States	0.72	
France	0.64	
Germany	0.66	
Italy	0.57	
United States–France	0.08	0.36
United States–Germany	0.06	0.31
United States–Italy	0.15	0.59
Weeks worked per year		
United States	46.16	
France	40.54	
Germany	40.57	
Italy	40.99	
United States–France	5.62	0.39
United Sates–Germany	5.59	0.44
United Sates–Italy	5.17	0.29
Usual weekly hours per worker		
United States	39.39	
France	36.21	
Germany	36.48	
Italy	37.42	
United States–France	3.18	0.25
United States–Germany	2.91	0.26
United States–Italy	1.97	0.13

Source: Alesina, Glaeser, and Sacerdote (2004).

goods and services from their homes, or they could be working in the black economy and not reporting income. There is ample evidence that some of the so-called European leisure activities are devoted to what economists call "household production." Think, for instance, of home-cooking versus restaurant meals, child care at home versus pre-school, and house cleaning. Of course, it is hard to say whether cooking is leisure or work, and the same applies to child care; probably it is a little of both. In some European countries, especially Italy, the black economy keeps occupied a fraction of the population reported as not working in the official statistics. This is important in the following sense. Imagine that the difference between the United States and Europe in measured working time could be captured by Europeans working at home and in the black economy. This would entirely eliminate the story that Europeans are simply more prone to enjoy leisure. Europeans could be working at home or in the black economy to avoid taxes and regulations, but they would do so less productively because productivity is higher with market specialization. So to the extent that Europeans do not work in the market because they work at home or in the black economy, the productivity of the economy is reduced. While it is unclear that home activities are always less productive then market activities (since home-cooked meals are healthier than take-outs from McDonald's), productivity loss is certainly the case for the black economy. Further, although home production and the black economy have something to do with lower hours worked in Europe, Europeans do indeed take more vacations than Americans. In August, for instance, even Parisians and Milanese in the black economy are not working.

Table 3.2 compares the work benefits of United States and Europe. As the table shows, a typical German worker works five and a half fewer weeks a year than an American worker. Of the remaining weeks, 4.8 weeks relate to the longer vacations due a worker in Germany, and add to that half a week more if the German worker

Table 3.2
Distribution of 52-week year into weeks worked, and not worked

	Annual weeks worked	Holidays and vacation weeks	Week-long absences for nonholiday reasons	Shorter absences for nonholiday reasons	Absences due to sickness and maternity leave
Austria	39.5	7.3	2.6	0.4	2.3
Belgium	40.3	7.1	2.2	0.5	2.0
Switzerland	42.6	6.1	1.5	0.7	1.1
Germany	40.6	7.8	1.8	0.3	1.5
Denmark	39.4	7.4	2.2	1.0	1.9
Spain	42.1	7.0	1.3	0.4	1.2
Finland	38.9	7.1	2.4	1.5	2.1
France	40.7	7.0	2.0	0.4	1.8
Greece	44.6	6.7	0.3	0.2	0.2
Hungary	43.9	6.3	0.9	0.1	0.8
Ireland	43.9	5.7	1.2	0.2	0.9
Italy	41.1	7.9	1.7	0.3	0.9
Luxembourg	41.9	7.5	1.3	0.1	1.1
Netherlands	39.6	7.6	2.0	0.8	2.0
Norway	37.0	6.5	4.0	1.1	3.5
Poland	43.5	6.2	1.2	0.3	0.9
Portugal	41.9	7.3	1.4	0.2	1.2
Sweden	36.0	6.9	3.8	1.7	3.7
United Kingdom	40.8	6.6	1.5	1.5	1.6
United States	46.2	3.9	0.94		0.96

Source: Alesina, Glaeser, and Sacerdote (2004). Original source: *OECD Employment Outlook* (2004, Sickness and maternity leave estimates are adjusted for 50 percent underreporting).
Note: For US data we calculate weeks of vacation and illness for full time heads in the PSID. We calculate weeks of holidays using federal and stock market holidays. Other nonholiday absences are accounted for in the residual.

chooses to report sick and another week if the worker chooses to be absent for some personal reason.

So why is it that Europeans choose to work less than Americans? As we have already mentioned, the first reason that comes to mind is taxes. Labor income taxes and, especially, marginal rates have been increasing in Europe since the mid-1970s, much more than in the United States. Europeans may work less because they are over-taxed: high taxes can induce people to take more leisure, move to the nontaxed black economy, or produce goods and services from their homes.

The scatter plot of figure 3.2 shows marginal labor income taxes and hours worked in several OECD countries, and the correlation appears to be strong. That is, as the tax rate goes up, the take-home wage goes down and people work less. In a widely cited paper

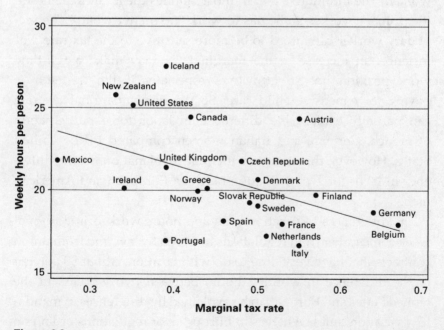

Figure 3.2
Decline in hours worked weekly and the rising marginal tax rate. Source: Alesina, Glaeser, and Sacerdote (2004)

Edward Prescott, the Nobel Prize winner for Economics in 2004, argued that the difference in hours worked between United States and Europe can be explained entirely by taxes.

There is no doubt that taxation has something to do with the propensity to work in the market (rather than work at home, in the black economy, or not work at all), but the question is whether taxes are the unique or even the main explanation of the US–Europe difference. The way to study this relationship is to observe how much people reduce their hours of work as their tax rates increase. In other words, how many more men and women will exit the labor force altogether or cut back on work hours as tax rates on income go up?

Labor economists have shown that the reaction of labor supply to changes in after-tax wages is small for men and higher for women. The intuition is that in most families the adult male is still the primary worker, so he has to work "no matter what." The secondary worker can afford to be more sensitive to the tax rate. For instance, an increase in the marginal tax may make a full-time work position not so attractive, especially if the trade-off is paying for expensive child care. So the rising marginal tax rate can partially explain the difference in labor force participation of French, German, and Italian women compared to the United States. However, this is not an adequate explanation for the difference in labor force participation between European and American men.

The differences in vacation time and hours worked in a normal week come rather from regulations imposed by law, and from union contracts that have very little to do with taxation. About 80 percent of the difference in working hours between two workers in the United States and Europe can be explained by differences in mandatory vacation times. Whereas in Europe labor regulations ordain no less than four vacation weeks a year, no such regulation exists in the United States. In addition, as we showed in figure 3.1, the decline in hours worked from the early 1970s onward presents a reasonably constant trend throughout the period, while tax increases were concentrated in the early part of the next three decades. For instance, the 35-hour week in France was introduced in 1999, not in a period of increasing tax rates.

Figure 3.3 shows the strong inverse correlation between the share of the labor force covered by union contracts and hours worked across the OECD. The evidence for the United States is consistent with the importance of labor unions in determining vacation time. Figure 3.4 shows a positive correlation between the number of vacation days and union density in US states. Also in the United States evidence drawn from individual surveys show that

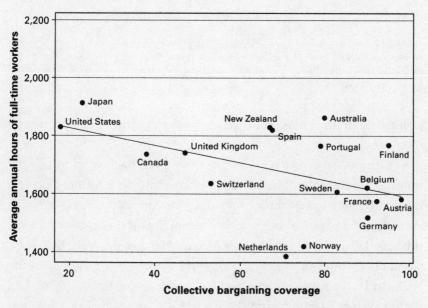

Figure 3.3
Percentage of hours worked annually covered by collective bargaining agreements.
Source: Alesina, Glaeser, and Sacerdote (2004)

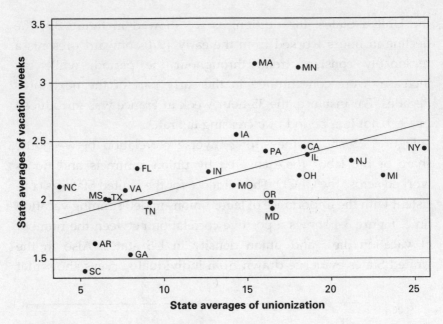

Figure 3.4
Average vacation time in the United States along with unionization rate, based
on data from the Bureau of Labor Statistics. Source: Alesina, Glaeser, and
Sacerdote (2004)

union members have more paid vacation time than nonunion
members.

In Europe the hours worked have been cut back over time, so if
union and labor regulations were responsible, their influence could
not have been so constant over time. Historically unions grew in
strength as a result of the political turmoil at the end of the 1960s,
the May 1968 riots in France, *Autunno caldo* in 1969 in Italy, the recession and turmoil of the early 1970s, the successes of the left in the
1970s in Italy and Germany, and in France in the early 1980s. As a
matter of fact, starting from the mid-1970s, at a time of increase in
unemployment, the slogan "Work less, work all" was chanted in
many different languages in European union marches. In France the
reduction of hours worked was the main battling grounds for

unions and the business owners in the 1970s. When the leftist government of Francois Mitterrand came into office in 1981, the political power shifted in favor of the unions and the 39-hour week was swiftly introduced.

Unions seemed to believe (or at least this was their rhetoric) that an economy can only provide a fixed number of hours to be divided among workers. By sharing this amount of work among more people, one could reduce unemployment. Work less, work all, precisely. But why did unions choose this strategy? One explanation is that in response to the shock of the early 1970s, unions fought to retain membership in declining industries by protecting union members from being laid off. So they pushed for policies of work sharing, and at the same time demanded equal pay for fewer hours. The increase in hourly wages led to an increase in labor costs and thus a reduction in labor demand, which increased unemployment and reduced even more the total hours worked.

Unions also had much influence in increasing the size of pension systems and lowering the average retirement age. This effect is particularly strong in Italy where an especially low fraction of older people (above age 55) are in the labor force. In some countries the younger generations stay in school longer, delaying entry into the labor force. Unions can be credited for this trend too, since they have often opposed temporary and more flexible labor contracts that could help younger and less qualified workers enter the labor force. Why? The answer is simple. Unions are run by older workers and even by retirees. They are more interested in protecting those categories, affecting their self-interests, than any younger cohort of workers.

Finally, as hours worked begin to fall, the process becomes self-sustaining. For every spouse, relative, friend, or co-worker who takes more vacation time, their enjoyment of the vacations went up as well, because the vacation time could be spent together with a spouse, relative, or friend. As friends stayed in school longer, and found they could take six weeks of vacation when they worked, others wanted to do the same and demanded more vacation time. Interestingly the evidence on Germany, as gathered by Jennifer Hunt, shows that as a member of a family obtained a new contract with more vacation time, the other member took more vacation too. Europeans like to enjoy vacations together, with family and friends.

This phenomenon is often referred to as a social multiplier: as the enjoyment of leisure increases with the number of people taking vacation time, the incentive rises for more people to take vacation time, and the average number of hours worked goes down. Cultural attitudes toward leisure slowly but surely evolve, and when it becomes the norm to have six-week vacations, a new social equilibrium is reached that is difficult to reverse. The same goes for retirement: when it becomes the norm for men to retire at sixty, workers approaching sixty do not want to continue working if they see people just a few years older already having enjoyed generous pensions for several years.

But there is more obvious evidence of the fact that other people's leisure increases our own. Think of the organization of the week days and weekends. From a production efficiency point of view it would make sense to run factories smoothly seven days a week. Vacation spots would not be overcrowded on weekends and empty on week days. Nevertheless, every modern society is organized with weekends.

So, is the reduction of work hours a cause of the sluggish growth rate in continental Europe in the last decade or so related to that in the United States? The short answer is yes. A longer answer requires discussion of labor productivity. At the end of the nineteenth century most of Europe was richer than the United States, although countries like Italy and Spain were much poorer. In the early 1950s, after two World Wars and the economic and political instability of the interwar years, output per capita in Europe had fallen to almost half the level in the United States. In the 1960s, and at a slower pace in the 1970s, Europe recovered some of the losses. As we mentioned in the Introduction, at the beginning of the 1980s European income per capita was 75 percent of the US level. Over the next 25 years, however, there were virtually no gains: the gap between output per capita in Europe and in the United States remained close to 25 percent. In other words, from the 1950s to the 1970s Europeans were working harder than Americans and were just as productive. They were also gaining ground. From the mid-1970s to the mid-1990s Europeans began to work less and less, but their rapid hourly productivity growth allowed them to keep pace with hard-working Americans. In the United States these were years of concern about slow productivity growth. For the last ten years, however, not only have Americans been working harder than Europeans, their productivity has been growing faster. Consequently Europe is falling behind. Clearly, if Europeans want to keep on working fewer hours, they had better start being even more productive when they work!

Still Europeans are satisfied and happy with their long vacations, early retirements, and short work weeks. Well, they certainly act as if they are. So far attempts at increasing work hours have met with much resistance. In Germany, for instance, a few years ago an opinion survey showed that German workers would work even fewer hours if they were given the option. Just the opposite is recorded in the United States: Americans declare themselves happy to work more for more pay if they have the opportunity. So, in sum, Europeans want to work even less and Americans are happy to work as much as they do, if not more. Interestingly there are signs that in some European countries this attitude is changing. Research by one of us (Giavazzi) has found that those Germans who are becoming uneasy about the sustainability of the welfare system are ready to accept cuts in vacation time and to increase their work hours significantly.

What will become of Europeans who choose to work less and less, to retire early, to eschew work, thereby raising taxes that pay for an expensive welfare state, and to opt for policies that discourage innovation and impede productivity? They will become poorer and poorer relative to harder working societies. As long as this is well understood . . . Europe, enjoy your holidays!

4

Job Security, Job Regulations, and 14 Million Unemployed

In the fifteen older EU member states, currently 14 million people are unemployed. Many economists believe that labor market rigidities, such as firing costs, union-imposed regulations on mobility within firms, and restrictions on overtime, reduce the flexibility with which employers can use labor, and are one of the main causes of European unemployment.

But the agreement pretty much stops here. In the one camp, there are those who believe that lack of labor market flexibility is by far the single most important problem of Europe and that it is the reason for Europe's relative stagnation, vis-à-vis the United States. In the other camp, there are those who believe that labor market rigidities do not increase unemployment per se but interfere with macroeconomic adjustments and thus allow unemployment to be persistent. Disagreement is even stronger when it comes to the question of what to do about unemployment. One camp believes that labor protection laws should be eliminated, making the market for labor like any other market. The other camp holds a more nuanced view that "European-style" legislation that protects workers from the ups and downs of the market should remain in place but be tweaked to minimize distortions and remove incentives to not work. In fact, as Ronald Reagan once said, "The best welfare program is a job!"

We subscribe to this latter view. Although labor market regulations have had a lot to do with creating high and persistent

European unemployment, it is near impossible politically and incorrect economically to dismantle all types of labor protection. From an economic perspective, unemployment insurance encourages individuals to participate in the labor market and not the black economy, which does not provide any insurance but is not taxed. Politically it is unthinkable that labor protection could simply be dismissed *tout court*. The most immediate issue is then how to reorganize a system of labor protection laws that does not discourage employment, both on the supply side (the workers) and on the demand side (the firms), and provides insurance to workers while not permanently increasing unemployment. How can one do that?

Let us start with firing costs. If a firm knows that it cannot fire its nonproductive employees, it must be very careful in its hiring practices. It must hire fewer workers or switch to labor-saving technologies, as many European firms did in the 1980s and 1990s. Obviously an insider, the worker who has a job, will favor retaining firing costs, but all those out of a job will lose out because of firing costs, since they will have a hard time gaining a job. Remember that despite their rhetoric against unemployment, unions' policies are geared toward the needs of elderly union members who have jobs.

A particularly pernicious firing cost is judicial intervention. In fact, not only does the law impose severe restrictions on firing, but even when employers follow the law, judges often step in and rule in favor of the workers. In France, for instance, judges rule routinely against any firing justified by the need to improve profitability of the firm. That is, increasing efficiency is not considered an acceptable justification to reduce employment in a firm. In Italy, when it comes to protecting employees against firing, the notoriously slow justice system is suddenly very fast and efficient, and many workers are promptly reinstated in their jobs.

Firing should be the prerogative of every firm. There are two types of firing: layoff of individual workers or small groups of workers, and closing of plants or even entire companies. Plant closings receive a lot of media attention (and union reaction), but as a fraction of total job flows, it is layoffs that constitute the larger contribution to unemployment. Both types are difficult decisions for European employers. Stories of absentee or even dishonest employees that cannot be dismissed are common—and for every absentee and dishonest worker that cannot be fired, a young, honest, and productive worker goes unemployed. In the other case, threats of closure of plants immediately generate a flow of subsidies and favors from the government to employers to bribe them into not firing. The result is of course that unproductive firms are kept alive instead of releasing workers to be reemployed in more productive sectors or enterprises.

This does not mean that the unemployed should go unprotected and that the labor market should function as the market for any other good. Unemployment causes loss of income for families, distress, and a variety of social problems. There is no question that the unemployed should receive insurance and that, since it is difficult for the private sector to insure them adequately, government should step in. Unemployment subsidies, however, should not discourage job search, as they currently often do, but rather they should encourage it. For instance, the subsidies should be ended if an unemployed person refuses a job offered to him or makes no effort to search for a job. Also unemployment compensation should not become permanent and/or be so generous and long-lasting that it becomes preferable to a job: it should only serve as an insurance scheme against temporary spells of unemployment.

The question is, of course, how to finance unemployment insurance. One option is from general government revenues, and this is the option most often followed. Two French economists, Olivier Blanchard of MIT and Jean Tirole of the University of Toulouse, have suggested an ingenious alternative. They proposed a "firing tax": firms could fire anyone they wanted to, but they would be taxed a certain amount, and this tax revenue would cover part of the government expenditure on unemployment subsidies. The reasoning is the following: if society bears the costs of unemployment, those who contribute to create it should properly "internalize" its costs and pay a tax for it. In other words, if the costs of unemployment are only borne by society, any firm can "overfire" because its employees will be compensated at no cost to the firm. Obviously the firing tax should be fixed at a level that is far less than prohibitive; otherwise, we are back to the problem of excessive rigidity! This system would also eliminate the inefficient involvement of judges in the hiring and firing process and would eliminate all (or most) regulations on firing. This proposal has been submitted to the French government, but it faces stiff opposition. One argument against it is precisely the alleged superiority of judges in determining when a firm can fire, a system that is deeply flawed.

Italy, until some recent reforms, had, together with France, one of the most inefficient labor markets. It was almost impossible to fire anyone for any reason and, at the same time, there were no unemployment subsidies. Exactly the opposite of what economic efficiency would call for! Recent labor market reforms have introduced new types of flexible labor contracts that are temporary and can be terminated very easily. Interestingly unemployment in Italy has been declining in the last few years (from 11 percent in the mid-1990s to 7.7 in 2005) despite low growth of the GDP. Much of this increase in employment happened thanks to these new contracts: for each traditional job (that is, a permanent job governed by the old rigid rules) there are seven new temporary contracts.

The problem of this reform is that is has created a two-tier system of workers—those with "standard" super-protected contracts, and the unprotected ones, which by now have reached 15 percent of total employment. The latter are typically younger workers who then find it difficult to enter the former type of contract. Because of the temporary nature of these contracts, however, employers have no incentive to train the employee, since this would imply retaining and moving the employee into the category of inflexible contracts. This is an imperfect system, and one that is probably responsible for the decline in the recent rate of Italian labor productivity growth.

Germany has also recently introduced labor market reforms, prompted by an extraordinary level of unemployment. In 2005 the number of people looking for jobs exceeded five million, the highest mark since January 1933 just before Hitler came to power. This means a national unemployment rate of 12.1 percent, with 20.5 percent seeking employment in the east and 10 percent in the west. The reforms adopted in 2005 are meant to encourage unemployed workers to accept jobs by reducing the generosity of unemployment benefits. Full benefits (65 percent of the previous net salary) previously lasted as long as three years; now they are limited to 12 months (18 months for the over-55-year-olds). After this an unemployed worker receives much lower welfare payments, provided that his income is above a given level. This means that half a million claimants (out of 2.1 million before the reforms) will no longer be eligible for any benefits at all. Also unemployed workers will from now on be forced to accept any job, no matter how below their expectation and below their qualification that job is. It is still too early to tell whether these reforms will be effective in reducing unemployment. One first effect they did have: Chancellor Schroeder, who has been responsible for pushing them through, was ousted a few months after the reform had been adopted—and he had run a campaign based on slowing down reforms.

Nordic countries have typically done better and come closer to the economically efficient systems sketched above. They have generous unemployment subsidies but low firing costs. The result is rates of unemployment that are much lower than in the rest of Europe and employment rates that are among the highest (see table 4.1).

Table 4.1
Unemployment rates and employment ratio, 2004

Country	Unemployment rate	Employed/population aged 15–64
Australia	5.5	71.3
Austria	4.8	64.7
Belgium	7.9	56.9
Canada	7.2	72.0
Denmark	5.4	76.9
Finland	9.0	66.9
France	9.6	62.3
Germany	9.5	65.7
Greece	10.5	59.2
Ireland	4.5	60.8
Italy	8.0	60.5
Japan	4.7	75.8
Netherlands	4.6	64.8
New Zealand	3.9	72.3
Norway	4.4	75.5
Spain	10.9	58.2
Sweden	6.4	78.0
Switzerland	4.4	74.8
United Kingdom	4.7	72.5
United States	5.5	72.8

Source: OECD Standardized Unemployment Rates, for Unemployment Rate, and World Development Indicators for Total Labor Force, Total Population, and Population Age 15–64.
Note: Total employed population is obtained by multiplying (100 – Unemployment) × Total labor force.

The best example is the so-called flex-security model adopted by Denmark. Among the European countries Denmark has the lowest firing costs and the most generous unemployment benefits system. The unemployed receive from the state 90 percent of their average earnings during the 12 weeks before they lose their jobs (with a cap beyond a certain level). And these benefits are provided for as long as 4 years and longer if the worker is close to retirement. To be eligible it is sufficient to have worked 52 weeks during the previous

3 years. To keep receiving these generous benefits, however, Danish unemployed workers must sign up for training programs and accept any job provided by the employment services. The first time they turn down a job offer, they lose the benefits. And jobs do come across easily, precisely because firing costs are low and firms can afford a mistake. The result is an unemployment rate of about 5.4 percent, well below the average in continental Europe.

Can the Nordic model be easily applied everywhere? This is not obvious. Two French economists Yarn Algan and Pierre Cahuc have shown that that much of the success of the Danish model has to do with a high degree of honesty in reporting and public spiritedness of Danes. When such cultural characteristics are absent in other (especially Mediterranean) countries, implementation of these schemes may be not as successful.

The bottom line is that the debate about labor market reforms in Europe should not be cast into the framework of a choice between no protection of workers and the existing legislation, no matter what it is. There are ways to combine labor protection and economic efficiency, by reducing the extent of the perverse effects on incentives. But, if this is the case, why is it often so difficult to implement this kind of efficiency-enhancing labor reform? As always, and this is a recurrent theme in this book, because a minority of privileged insiders often have enough power to block these reforms. In this case it is the unions that are run by, and therefore interested in, older employed workers with safe jobs. Reducing firing costs would be especially beneficial for new entrants into the job market and more generally for all those not in the labor force. It would not favor older workers who could now get fired more easily. Why their interests should take precedence over those of the young, the unemployed, and discouraged workers who left the labor force is a mystery to us. In truth, it is not a mystery, it is a sign of how successful unions have been, and it indicates a need to curtain their political influence.

To be sure, unions do have a role to play in a democratic society. The problem is that they often go beyond their duty of representing employees with employers and abuse the system. In many countries, unions have taken on a political role. They sit at many government tables and bargain directly over economic policy. In some cases, again especially in the Nordic countries, unions have often helped achieve consensus. But more often in other countries unions have blocked reforms for reasons that did not seem to match the general interests of society. In many situations, if an agreement is not reached, often the unions can block policy implementation. In 1994 a general strike in Italy toppled a government that was trying to introduce a pension reform with union consent. One of the provisions of this reform was to increase the retirement age of those workers who had a right to retire with full benefits in their mid-fifties. Not surprisingly, this was the group of workers for whom union membership was the highest. France in 2003 had to endure a month of social unrest and unrelenting strikes when the government introduced a relatively minor pension reform that withdrew some retirement privileges for public employees.

European governments should have the courage to stand up to unions that behave like lobbies and defend relatively privileged groups of workers. They should unmask the rhetoric that unions like to use, about their alleged defense of the underprivileged. Where unions have veto power over government policies, we can expect very little progress in reforms.

5 Technology, Research, and Universities

Why should Europeans concern themselves with innovation? Couldn't they simply imitate the technological breakthroughs achieved elsewhere? After all, the success of Japan and Korea has been based almost entirely on their extraordinary ability to imitate the United States, and even Europe in the 1960s advanced largely thanks to the adoption of technologies developed across the Atlantic.

Imitation is no longer enough for Europe. Imitation works when a country is still far from the technological frontier. As the research by Philippe Aghion, Daron Acemoglu, and Fabrizio Zilibotti shows, countries that are far away from the frontier can pursue an imitation-based strategy, but closer to the technology frontier there is less room for copying and adoption of well-established technologies. So it is important to establish innovation-enhancing institutions and policies.

This observation has important implications for the European debate over industrial policy. As the examples of Korea and Japan show, imitation works well for large firms, a bank-centered financial system, long-term relationships, a slow turnover of managers, and a hands-on approach by the government. In Japan, the Ministry of International Trade and Industry (MITI) played a crucial role in industrial activity by regulating import licenses, and the extent of competition, and by encouraging investment by the *keiretsu*, large groupings of industrial firms and banks. In the Korean case, the large family-run conglomerates, the *chaebol*, have been important in generating large investments and rapid technological development. The chaebol too received strong government support in the form of subsidized loans, anti-union legislation, and protection from competition.

In Europe, there are some analogies. The French public administrators trained in the Ecole National d'Administration can shift from government jobs to running large companies in a circuit fairly close to outsiders. Italy's growth in the postwar years and up to the late 1960s owes a lot to IRI, a government-owned industrial conglomerate that controlled half of the country's manufacturing activities and many of the largest banks, and produced a generation of good managers. This contributed to Europe's success up to the 1970s. Today Europe is closer to the technological frontier where innovation is the critical factor for growth, but Europe is ill prepared to innovate. The very institutions that were responsible for the successes of the 1960s are today hindrances to growth.

Even the conditions for successful imitation have changed—assuming Europe still wants to exploit imitation. A greater proportion of today's innovations are radical rather than elemental. Adopting them requires the ability to make big changes in the way firms are organized. In a sense, today's ICT (Information and communication technology) innovations are similar to the introduction of the electrical engine in the textile industry at the beginning of the last century. Electrical engines had been available since the 1890s, but it took almost thirty years before the new technology could start increasing productivity. The main reason was the profound changes in the organization of factories that the electrical engine required and the resistance of unions to accept them. As we will discuss in a moment, a big difference between American and European companies is the ability to change the organization of the firm fast enough to adapt it to new technologies. The slower a firm adapts, the longer it takes for the new technology to raise productivity.

At the technological frontier the vital instruments are, first, excellent universities with the ability to attract the best minds, and second, a business environment with lots of "creative destruction," that is, an environment where defunct firms can close down and new firms replace them, since it is mostly in the new firms that technology is developed. Europe lags behind in both dimensions. We defer the discussion of why there is little creative destruction to the next chapter—it is essentially lack of competition and too many state subsidies that keep incumbent firms alive and make it more difficult for new firms to enter. Here we concentrate on the development of technology and the ability to implement it.

The United States has a clear edge in high-tech firms. Its comparative advantage in the high-tech industries (aircraft, pharmaceuticals, computers, and TLC equipment, medical and optical instruments) has sharpened over the past fifteen years. In Europe only the United Kingdom has a comparative advantage in the high-tech sectors. France and Germany specialize in more traditional industries (chemicals, cars and trucks, electrical machinery) and Spain and Italy in low-tech sectors (such as textiles, which is now threatened by China). Rather then competing for the best minds, European universities go out of their way to protect insiders. So Europe ends up exporting many of its brightest students to America, while the brightest students from India and from Central and Eastern Europe fly over Paris on their way to Boston, Chicago, or California.

But there is more to it than simply the fact Europe lags behind in the high-tech industries. As new technology becomes available, a firm must be able to apply it in ways that increase productivity. That is, firms must be flexible enough to be able to adapt their production and sales plans. In the United States the technological innovations of the 1990s came after a decade of restructuring: the leverage buyouts of the 1980s had changed the style of the American corporation. Firms bought with debt had to be trimmed down, restructured, cut in pieces. This required a strong chief executive officer (CEO) and a culture that had no other objective than the bottom line. Adapting the firms to the new technologies was often insignificant compared with what they had lived through in the 1980s. Thus change came fast.

In the 1980s, while so-called barbarians were restructuring US corporations, European firms were coddled by the state with subsidies and protection from outside competition. With large rents, there was little pressure put on CEOs to ensure in return economic efficiency and maximum productivity. Tyrannical CEOs capable of turning around the organization of a firm almost overnight were rare in Europe. European firms typically were elaborately structured to allow for lengthy consensus building in decision-making. At the extreme was the case of supervisory boards in large German firms where union representatives take up half the seats—obviously a governance structure hardly conducive to producing organizational changes. At Volkswagen, for instance, the shareholders had to bribe union leaders on the supervisory board and provide them with luxury trips to get their agreement on changes to working rules. Although as the Enron case has demonstrated, American CEOs can likewise succumb to greed, the sharp competition among CEOs, due to their extraordinarily high salaries, ensures that mistakes are dearly paid for at least in lost jobs.

Deregulation was also an important factor in the weakening of American unions. As we discussed in chapter 4, unions often protect current employees at the expense of the unemployed. Street marches of unions against closures of plants or factories are still common in Europe. In their defense of employment, few—and certainly not the unions of the insiders—

are willing to acknowledge that closures and restructurings of plants often lead to overall employment increases. Admittedly new job openings come after a period of adjustment, but welfare programs could be designed to smooth these costs. Thus currently Europe not only lags behind in the development of new technologies but also does not provide an environment friendly to their adoption.

Let us turn to universities. In general, with very few exceptions, European universities are based on four misconceived ideas: taxpayers rather than students and grants and donations from the private sector pay for university education; faculty appointments are governed by public sector contracts; laws and university procedures are centralized and not be very flexible; and salaries among teachers are equalized, with a more or less clearly stated policy goal to equalize the quality of teaching and research among universities.

Europeans are becoming aware that their universities are by and large losing ground. Nevertheless, the discussion on universities in Europe is full of misperceptions that have led policy-making in the wrong direction. Not surprisingly, European academics have an incentive to perpetuate myths about the lack of resources. The standard argument heard around academic dinner tables in Europe is that salaries are miserable and there is no money for research. Neither is true. Even if these were true, throwing more money without changing archaic university rules would produce more waste, not more research output. In today's Europe the university system is mostly a bastion of power, prestige, and a wealth of entrenched lobbies of university professors who prevent entry of young gifted academics and thus competition.

As table 5.1 shows, some data bring the point home. The data are taken from the research of Roberto Perotti of Bocconi University, which compares Italian and British universities. The comparison is particularly useful because British universities are considered to be

Table 5.1
State expenditures on British and Italian universities in US dollars

	United Kingdom 1998–1999	Italy 1999–2000
Spending on academic staff	138,977	162,532
Spending on student	9,125	6,697
Spending on FTE student	12,435	16,854
Spending on nonacademic staff	45,394	57,962

Source: R. Perotti (2002: The Italian university system: Rules vs. incentives. Working paper).

the best in Europe and Italian universities among the worst, and with fewer resources. Expenditures on students and faculty are, however, very close in the two systems, and even slightly higher in Italy. The distinction between full-time students and total number of students is critical in Italy, which, unlike the United Kingdom, supports a very large number of so-called students who never go to class, take one or two exams a year, and remain registered until their late twenties or early thirties. They are basically the hidden unemployed. Spending on university staffs is also much higher in Italy than in the United Kingdom.

Table 5.2 shows the number of students per faculty and staff. There are about as many full-time students per faculty in the United Kingdom as in Italy. The fact that more research comes out of the UK universities therefore cannot be attributed to Italian professors being overburdened by teaching loads or by number of students. As a result the research coming out of British universities is at a much lower cost than that of Italy.

As table 5.3 shows, an academic paper costs society almost twice as much in Italy than in the United Kingdom. Further British professors are twice as productive as Italian professors and are cited much more often.

Clearly, lack of resources is not the main reason why European universities lag behind. Still discussions in Europe about research

Table 5.2
Ratios of student to faculty in 1999

	United Kingdom	Italy
Full-time students per academic staff	11.0	11.2
Without graduate students	9.3	10.4

Source: Perotti (2002).

Table 5.3
Cost of research in Italy and United Kingdom

	United Kingdom	Italy
Papers per US$ million, 1997	16.0	9.0
Citations per US$ million, 1997	70.5	34
Papers per professor, 1997	11.2	5.6
Citation per paper, 1994–1998	4.5	3.8

Source: Perotti (2002).

and universities typically start with a call for more public funding for public universities. Take the example of the recommendation of the Sapir Report. This influential document was prepared by a group of European economists for the European Commission and received wide attention. The implicit equation underlying the funding argument is: More money brings more research and better teaching. Not necessarily. Far more important is reform of the incentive structure for professors and students to engage in good research and good teaching. (We will return to the Sapir Report in the final chapter of this book.)

Europe's tendency to equalize salary and treatment of professors and researchers reduces the incentive to excel. If the only factor that increases a professor's salary is the passage of time, why should the professor make that extra effort? To be sure, some research is expensive, and top researchers are expensive. But competition is the time-tested factor that can re-distribute existing resources and raise results from mediocrity to excellence. Achieving excellence means attracting private funding for research, and it will mean charging students and their families higher tuition commensurate with better education.

The university situation in the United States is different. Take an American economics PhD considering entry into the academics field. Ex ante he or she faces lots of uncertainty. The salary as an assistant professor can be as high as US$170,000, if he is hired by the highest paying business school, and as low as $50,000 if he only finds a job teaching in a small liberal arts college. Whatever job he takes, if his productivity does not change, by simply waiting his salary will increase only marginally. At the end of his career he will be making only 1.5 times what he made as an assistant professor. Consider instead an Italian academic. All entry jobs pay the same, admittedly not so high, salary. But once entered into the system, by simply lying back and waiting, at the end of his career an academic's salary increases by as much as 3.7 times the beginning salary. Perotti calculates that at age 60 the salary of an Italian full professor is—independent of his productivity—higher than the salary of 80 percent of US tenured professors teaching in a university with a graduate program and of 95 percent of those teaching in a university that does not offer graduate degrees. So much for the lousy pay.

The difference lies in the structure of incentives. There in no ex ante uncertainty in Italy, and therefore there is no incentive to work hard. In the United States, on the contrary, the ex ante uncertainty is large and so are the incentives. In Italy once you are in you are in forever. At the time of this writing there has been an attempt at reforming the Italian system. A sort of tenure system has been proposed whereby researchers (equivalent to assistant professors) are to be evaluated in six years from employment. The proposal, however, has generated a revolt of current researchers who demand job security from the very moment they were hired.

Let us turn next to the cost of tertiary education, our second point. In Europe taxpayers, rather than the students, pay for university education. This system is supposedly more egalitarian than America's system of higher education, which many Europeans look down on as elitist. However, Europe's system produces less research, worse students (especially at the doctoral level), and is probably not more egalitarian than the US system. Having taxpayers cover the costs of university education may be redistributive, but it is redistribution in the wrong direction—the beneficiaries are most often children of families with relatively high incomes. To take a generous view, the best that can be said is that the system is neutral insofar as redistribution is concerned, since the wealthiest pay more taxes and use more university services. Several years ago one of the authors of this book gave a week-long lecture course in Helsinki for a European PhD program attended by students from all over Europe. A group of graduate students from Denmark participated. The Danish government (namely Danish taxpayers) supported their attendance with: four-star hotel accommodation, an equivalent of US$100 a day for expenses (this was the early 1990s), and business class air travel.

In addition to favoring Europe's "haves," this system makes it virtually impossible for self-financed private universities to survive, and this may even be why free public universities exist: to perpetuate the state's monopoly on higher education. Consider, instead, the US system. US students pay for their education, and with part of the tuition, universities finance scholarships for deserving students from poor families. Such a system is at least as fair as Europe's model, and probably more so than one in which taxpayers pay for everybody, including the rich. In fact recent research comparing education in the United States and Italy points to family income as more important in determining a student's success (measured in terms of earning power) in "egalitarian" Italy than it is in "elitist" America. What is interesting in the debate in Europe is that the proposals on making students pay for their tuition (with fellowships for the less well off) are automatically viewed as favoring the rich

and dismissed by parties on the right as well as on the left as political anathema. Even in Britain, Tony Blair's move in this direction
almost cost him his job, and in many ways it turned out to be a more
difficult decision than his support of the war in Iraq.

Observing how adamant Europeans are in support of the near
monopoly of public education at the tertiary level shows how deeply
rooted in Europe are anti-market sentiments. Using the words "competition" and "education" in the same sentence in most European
circles is considered not only wrong, but crass. In the United States,
in contrast, public and private universities coexist and compete
happily. The University of California at Berkeley is public; Stanford
University, an hour away down the coast, is private. Both are excellent universities. Competition between them works because it
involves fighting for the best researchers and the best students and
offering scholarships to deserving students. Very few Europeans
would guess that Berkeley is public and Stanford private because
they seem similar for all practical purposes: they compete for the
same faculty, they offer similar salaries, similar teaching loads, and
they are organized similarly.

By contrast, and this speaks to our third point above, Europe's
centralization and bureaucratic control over universities has often
produced mediocrity. Appointments in European universities are
almost universally governed by complex processes that involve
countless "judges" chosen from all over the country. This process is
supposedly designed to guarantee that the best are appointed. In
reality these judges make it easier for insiders to appoint their
friends, rather than for the quality of research and teaching to determine who is hired. This is a typical example of the flawed European
approach to regulation. If the goal is to guarantee quality, then
making competition possible is the obvious and best strategy.
Instead of embracing competition, European legislators keep trying
to improve their universities by producing new rules that are meant

to correct the failings of the previous generation of rules. This is not the way to change.

Some data on the effects of lack of competition come from an analysis of Italian appointments in economics by Roberto Perotti, who shows that "insider" status nearly always assures success. It would take an outsider thirteen refereed publications to make up for the advantage an insider has. Thirteen is a very large number; in the last round of competition, the average number of journal publications of the participants was seven. Some countries, such as France, are changing their systems by inviting academics from other countries to sit on hiring and promotion committees. While this is obviously a move in the right direction, it can produce few results. The best American universities operate their hiring internally, relying on outsiders only for expert opinions on the quality of a candidate's research. What produces good appointments is the threat that mediocre professors will make it difficult to attract good students and large research grants. It is competition that ensures quality.

Incentives, once again, are key. In Europe salaries are not differentiated by productivity. Low salaries at the beginning of a university career are part of an implicit bargain: in exchange for the bad pay whoever is hired automatically gets tenure. So there is no need to produce quality research. Also since the salary is low, university administrators close their eyes to lazy teaching and poor research, and deans do not stop their faculty members from scouring the country to do lucrative consulting, which is a major distraction from research. The result is bad teaching, lousy research, and absentee professors. Further, as professors age, their university salaries rise and become quite high. So many elderly stay on as absentee professors, continue in their consulting, and draw a very decent salary.

By contrast, American universities often use aggressive financial incentives and differential treatment of professors to reward good

teaching and research. The private nature of contracts between an
American university and its professors creates healthy competition
for talent and a flexible and efficient market for scientists. The result
is that it is not uncommon for a dynamic, productive young professor in America to earn more than more senior but less productive colleagues.

It should be no surprise then that nowadays American universities are being increasingly staffed by some of Europe's best
scholars. What is surprising in the face of this brain drain is the
powerful lobby of university professors in Europe to block reform.
Often the economics professors among them pontificate on the benefits of competition in product markets, but they strategically close
their eyes to the absolute lack of competition in their own academic
market.

Academic careers, aside, is the claim true that in Europe there is
no money to carry out research? Total spending on research and
development *is* lower in Europe than in the United States, but not
by an enormous amount. In the 1990s the United States devoted to
R&D 2.8 percent of GDP annually, compared with 2.3 percent in
Germany, 2 percent in the United Kingdom, and 1.9 percent in
France. European governments typically complain about the lack of
fiscal resources to support R&D (a far-fetched argument given the
miniscule share of research spending in the oversized European
budgets).

Another myth is that innovative firms must be nurtured and subsidized if they are to survive (see below in chapter 7). Whenever the
European Commission allows them, European governments subsidize innovative firms, or those that they think are more likely to
invest in R&D. This strategy, however, is unlikely to boost the European high-tech sector because weakness in R&D research is not—
at least not primarily—a funding issue. Europe trails the United
States in every dimension: the number of patents, the number of
Nobel laureates, and the number of researchers it is able to attract

from the rest of the world. Counting Nobel laureates by the country where most of their research was carried out, and only considering science laureates (medicine, chemistry, and physics) from 1945, to 2003, the United States has 193 laureates, the United Kingdom 44, Germany 23, Switzerland 18, France and Sweden 10 each, the former Soviet Union 9, and Japan 7. The supremacy of the Anglo-American system is striking. Data concerning patents e vidence America's advantage: in the late 1990s, 56 percent of all global patents in high-tech fields were granted to US applicants, while only 11 percent went to EU applicants. The connection between R&D and growth is too obvious to doubt that Europe's sluggish economies are a direct result of European backwardness innovation.

Funding is only part of the problem. A euro spent on research in Europe is less productive than a dollar spent in the United States for two reasons: incentives and demand for technology. We discussed incentives with reference to academics. But where demand for science comes from is also an important factor in determining the right incentives. Demand for technology helps focus research, provides deadlines, screens the output, and allows patents to be valued at market prices. Without the incentives provided by those at the receiving end, research risks drifting along without clear direction. Admittedly this is not true in all fields: the study of ancient Greek codices is valuable even it hardly meets any demand. But it has been important in certain theoretical and applied fields that have furthered the development of technologies in physics, biology, chemistry, and engineering.

Defense spending is a major factor in the demand for research. Most technological breakthroughs in the postwar period—from microchips to the Internet to the new batteries for cellular phones (developed for the US Army in Iraq) had, at least initially, a military application. Cell phones, satellite tracking, and high-resolution cameras were not cheap to come by, but happily for the industries that use them, costs for their development were partly picked up by the US government.

The superiority of the United States in research is largely due to the size and the composition of expenditure on defense. The US Pentagon's budget is not simply big: it accounts for more than one-half of *all* US government spending on research and development. European defense budgets are so very small in comparison, and they are divided. Europe's inability to create a unified defense budget, until very recently, is a big reason why it lags behind the United States in R&D. In 2001, however, there was a first positive sign. In response to an ongoing dispute between Europe and the United States over the choice of the military transport plane—to be used to deploy the new 60,000 strong European Rapid Reaction Force—a major milestone was reached. While America lobbied Europe to opt for an aircraft built by Boeing and Lockheed Martin, the aerospace industries of European NATO came together in a partnership to launch the Airbus Military A-400 M. The contract signed, in May 2003, between Airbus Military and OCCAR (Organ-isation Conjointe de Coopération en Matière d'Armement) for a total of 180 aircraft included representatives from Belgium, France, Germany, Luxembourg, Spain, Turkey, and the United Kingdom. The first flight of the A-400 M will be in 2008 and the first delivery in 2009.

In summary, discussions about research and universities in Europe almost always begin (and end) with a call for more public funds. This is not right. Far more important is reform of the incentive structure in European universities and in the private sector to develop new technologies. Moreover, in the hiring of educators and researchers, more competition rather than more public funds support is the way to ensure this progress.

6

Competition, Innovation, and the Myth of National Champions

In Europe incumbent firms enjoy large rents. They rarely close down, and potential entrants face high barriers. That is, many inefficient firms do not exit the market and too few new efficient enterprises are created to replace them. The result is that there is insufficient innovation and no "creative destruction" by which the natural disappearance of less efficient firms leaves room for more efficient ones.

Rather than encouraging creative destruction, European governments provide incumbent firms with state subsidies, in the wrong belief that government grants to firms advance innovation. Indeed one of the first economic decisions by the new German Chancellor Angela Merkel was to spend 25 million euros on subsidies to firms and on infrastructure investment in the hope that this will spur innovation and growth.

Think back to the IBM of the 1970s. It was the threat posed by the success of Apple that convinced IBM to speed up the introduction of the personal computer. Because Apple was able to enter the market, and the US government did not subsidize IBM, the IBM PC would come into production a few years later.

Some of the ideas in this chapter draw upon O. Blanchard and F. Giavazzi, 2003, Macroeconomic effects of regulation and deregulation in goods and labor markets, *Quarterly Journal of Economics*, August.

There are three good reasons why Europe lacks creative destruction. *Regulations* that create large rents by making it costly for more efficient firms to enter a market, *government subsidies to incumbents*, and *weak antitrust authorities*. In a word, lack of competition.

We begin with a small but revealing example of how regulation works to distort incentives. Taxi drivers are relatively well off in many European cities, where a taxi ride costs much more than in New York. The fact that gas costs less in the United States (because taxes on gasoline are lower) is a small part of the problem. The real reason is that the number of licenses is strictly controlled. While this is true in most United States cities as well, taxi drivers in many European cities have managed to obtain more stringent regulations that prohibit the operation of unlicensed cars and van services (for instance, a driver who holds a license often cannot hire a second driver, so the taxi remains garaged half the time). With market entry blocked, license owners face little pressure to hold down fares, and the officials who allocate licenses are well placed to collect votes or bribes. In short, regulation stimulates what economists call rent-seeking behavior: the taxi driver and the license official collect unearned premiums (rents) solely because they can exploit their position as insiders, not because they are more productive.

Zoning is another example of regulation. In Europe zoning prevents the creation of large distribution centers. In food distribution large establishments account for just 20 percent of all shops in Italy, and 25 percent in Germany, as opposed to 60 percent in Britain (This is an area where France, with a 53 percent share of large establishments, is closer to Britain than it is to Germany and Italy.) Claiming to protect the environment and the tradition of European cities, these regulations are really protecting the rich at the expense of the poor, and allowing small shopkeepers to hang on to large rents. While protecting the tradition and architectural beauty of European cities is a worthy goal for many reasons (including tourism), Europe hardly needs 70 percent of retail trade being held by small shop-keepers to achieve this goal. But, of course, shopkeepers want people to believe that!

Moreover, small shopkeepers seem to be the darlings of European politicians, and they have managed to generate much sympathy from the public despite their high prices compared to supermarkets. In many places shop opening hours are tightly regulated to pre-vent another margin of competition. Even where these regulations have been lifted, they survive, perhaps by custom but more likely because shopkeepers collude. Try to shop at 2 pm in most European cities outside of major tourist centers: you will find that all shopkeepers are out to lunch. Office workers looking to shop on their lunch break are out of luck. Need to go to the bank on Saturday morning? Forget it. Banks are closed on Saturdays, and on week days banks stay open only until 3 pm or 4 pm. Need to buy a newspaper in Milan on a Sunday afternoon? All newsstands are closed, and newspaper publishers don't think to set up small metal boxes at street corners for people to buy the paper whenever they feel like it. The newsstand owners' lobby may protest. If you are elderly and should happen to get sick on a weekend, the only place that can sell you an aspirin is a pharmacy, but again only a few phar-macies are open on weekends. So you will end up paying rent to two people, the pharmacist and the taxi driver who drives you there.

Next is the example of rent extracted by the notary public. Try to buy a used car in a European country. In most European countries, if you think that once you survived the used car dealer you are home, you are wrong. The next thing you have to do is stand in line for a couple of hours and pay a rent to the only person authorized to do this transaction, a notary public. In Europe notary publics are as pervasive as lawyers are in the United States, but there is a subtle difference. In the United States you can buy a house from your brother and, if you trust him, take the risk and do the transaction without a lawyer—not in Europe. Going through a notary public is compulsory in Europe. Further, entry into the notary business is restricted, so there are very few notaries and they can charge high fees.

Subsidies are another subtle way governments curtail competition. In 2004 the French government sought to save Alstom from going bust. The self-proclaimed "liberalist" Sarkozy engineered this operation. Alstom is a large conglomerate that developed a number of very successful high-tech products, including the TGV, the French fast train, but had come close to bankruptcy after having lost €3.5 billion between 2001 and 2004. The losses had mostly come from outdated plants (shipbuilding and power generation systems) situated in northern France that were politically impossible to close down. The logical solution was to break up the firm: sell the profitable TGV and close the unprofitable plants. French taxpayers' money could be better spent on temporary benefits for displaced workers than on subsidies to keep unprofitable plants alive. This is not what happened: the entire company was kept afloat with public grants. In April 2006 the state relinquished its share of Alstom to (surprise!) a French group, Bouygues. The cost for France has been not just the inefficiency associated with keeping alive plants that should have been closed down; the additional cost is that it becomes hard to tell whether profitable plants are really profitable, or whether they turn a profit only because some subsidies enable them to do so. The existence of subsidies creates confusion in market perception and makes it difficult for potentially profitable competitors to enter the market.

Table 6.1 lists the French attempts at creating national champion firms in technology. The subsidies came not only in the form of the direct government grants shown in the table but also through government contracts and programs reserved to prevent competition from non-French firms. The data in the table, but not

Table 6.1
Government grants to French "national champions," 1960 to 1990

Name of the program	Start date	R&D area	Name of the firm	Government grant
Concorde	1962	Electronic flight equipement	Aérospatiale	€3.9 billion between 1970 and 1990
Plan Calcul	1996	Computers	UNIDATA e Bull	€8 billion
Nucléaire civil	1968	Nuclear	CEA, EDF	NA
Airbus	1969	Aerospace	Aérospatiale e Airbus	€3 billion at the start
Spatial	1973	Ariane missile	Aérospatiale e Air Liquide	NA
Réacteurs	1973	Engines for Airbus	CFMSG	NA
Train à Grande Vitesse	1974	Fast speed trains	Alstom	€2.1 billion for the first TGV line
Minitel	1978	Telephones	France Telecom	€1.2 billion for PTT
Plan composants	1989	Microchips	Thomson, diventata ST Microelectronics	NA

Source: Data from a report prepared for the French government by J.-L. Beffa (2005: *Pour une nouvelle politique industrielle*, Paris).

the programs, stop in 1990. EDF, the French electricity monopoly, has recent exploited its privileged position in France (due to the advantage it enjoyed in having installed nuclear reactors three decades ago) to buy up power plants throughout Europe, among them London Electricity and Edison, Italy's second large producer.

Who pockets the rents when competition is lacking? Rents are often split among four entities: the firm's owner, management, and workers, and sometimes politicians or public administrators

who have the power to grant licenses. Not surprisingly, all
four collude to protect their portion of the rent from competition.
In the gas and electricity industries, for example, unions are
the most stubborn opponents of opening the industries to
competition.

The costs imposed by lack of competition go beyond the inefficiency created in the product market. For instance, they distort the
incentives of entrepreneurs, inducing them to shift to businesses
that are protected and produce large, easy to grab rents, and to
abandon more risky projects. Consider the case of Benetton,
the well-known Italian textile firm. Years back Benetton was an
innovative firm, which had conquered the world market with a
smart business idea: all sweaters produced were gray and
dyed only after an order had come in from the shops. When a
season ends, traditional firms typically discard half their production, but Benetton could keep a sweater in stock for a number of
years. Then the Italian government decided to privatize the highways. To lure investors, it offered a sweet deal by committing to relatively high tolls. The smart Benetton family saw the dollar bills
lying on the floor and rapidly shifted from textiles to running the
highways. Moving out of textiles was the right thing to do for a
company based in an industrial country. But those smart entrepreneurs, instead of using their skills to develop a new business idea,
now use them to lobby politicians and make sure the tolls remain
high.

The bottom line is that the absence of competition produces too
little destruction of inefficient firms and too little creation of new
firms. Scholars of innovation have found that subsidies reduce
rather than speed up the pace of innovation. Productivity growth
arises from the destruction of the old and creation of the new. Subsidizing research and development of incumbent companies does
not lead to innovation but rather to rents. Take the case of Fiat. Over

a period of fifty years the Italian government spent many GDP points to subsidize its R&D. But instead of using the money to innovate, Fiat decided to diversify. It bought insurance companies and energy firms, all well-protected activities. Meanwhile its competitors were focused on improving the quality of their cars. So one day Fiat managers looked up and saw that they had lost Fiat's market share and that bankruptcy was around the corner.

Recently a document was issued by the European Commission on the mistaken view that state aid is the way to promote innovation. "Research and innovation generally thrive best in open and competitive markets. However, market failure may hamper the delivery of optimal levels of research and innovation. State aid can tackle market failures and change the incentives of market participants, thus facilitating research and innovation. While existing rules already provide wide possibilities for Member States to support research and innovation through State aid, the Commission has announced that it will review its rules to better reflect Community policy priorities and the need for a more research and innovation-friendly system." Moreover, Gunter Verheugen, the commissioner for industry and vice president of the Barroso commission, was fast to add that in the case of "European champions" antitrust and state aid rules should be applied with caution. So governments are being encouraged to intervene by promoting grandiose industrial policy projects.

Following the suggestion of a committee chaired by Jean Louis Beffa, the CEO of Saint Gobain, France created a special *Agence pour l'Innovation* whose purpose, thanks to a 6 billion euro government grant, is to support the "industrial projects of the future." Within the traditional dirigisme of French administration, this agency is supposed to select incumbent firms and assign them the task of developing new projects in areas identified by the bureaucrats who will run the *Agence*. This strategy is certain to fail. One has only to recall the experience of twenty years ago when Paris decided to turn Crédit Lyonnais, a French bank, into the world's largest financial institution outside of Japan. The plan failed and the bank had to be rescued, with the taxpayer footing a bill amounting to a few percentage points of France's GDP. The attempt to create a French computer champion by subsidizing Bull is still ongoing, and no one has yet added up the bills—the last bill, in the summer of 2004, was for half a billion euros.

At this point Europeans, and the French in particular, point at the success of Airbus and the French fast trains, TGV. The Airbus company has clearly been a success, winning a market share that has overtaken that of Boeing. But how large is the bill that European taxpayers have footed in the forty years since the company was created? No one really knows. What we know is that Airbus's current plan to build the A380 Superjumbo will cost €12 billion. The government grant that will pay for this project is unlikely ever to the paid back. At a price per plane of €200 million, and assuming a 15 percent mark up on variable costs, Airbus would need to sell 360 planes to pay back the grant (assuming zero interest—an unlikely target considering that in thirty-five years the 747 planes Boeing has sold number only 1,400). One would need a tremendous increase in travelers, which is not impossible if a billion or more Chinese and Indians become rich enough. But the important point is that Airbus is a unique example. Aircraft manufacturing is the only industry where economies of scale are so large that Europe and the United States can only support a single producer each. When this happens, governments cannot resist the perverse incentive to subsidize production—since the US government too subsidizes Boeing—in order to affect the outcome of the competitive game and shift rents in favor of the domestic firm. Aircraft manufacturing, we repeat, is a unique example.

Recall our discussion of technology and innovation in chapter 5, where we compared the imitation and innovation models of growth and explained why imitation was a good model for Europe in the 1960s and 1970s but one that no longer works. Trains and passenger aircrafts are relatively established technologies. In a sense they are the last examples of what Europeans were good at in the 1960s and 1970s—adapting and improving technologies developed elsewhere, and in the United States in particular. Like Toyota, which adapted American technology and eventually became the world's largest and most successful car producer, Airbus started by copying Boeing and McDonnell Douglas and eventually overtook both companies. Again, it is a case of excellent imitation rather than innovation. It would be interesting to know how much of the electronic and software technology built inside an Airbus (probably the most innovative components of a plane) is European as opposed to bought in the United States.

The inefficiencies created by the lack of competition in the product and service markets have a way of trickling down to the labor market. Where a firm collects large rents, unions have the incentive to fight hard and grab a fraction of those rents. As figure 6.1 shows, there is a strong positive correlation across countries between the extent of competition in the product market and the extent to which legislation protects workers, thus raising their power in negotiations with the firms. Wage bargaining is mostly about the distribution of rents between the firm and its workers. In a competitive industry, where there are no rents, there is little to extract in wage bargaining and therefore less incentive for unions to bargain.

The lesson is that there is an additional and more subtle way of introducing flexibility into European labor markets, besides the direct way we examined in chapter 4. The way to liberalize the labor market may be to start with the product market and eliminate the rents. Consider the railway industry, which in most European coun-

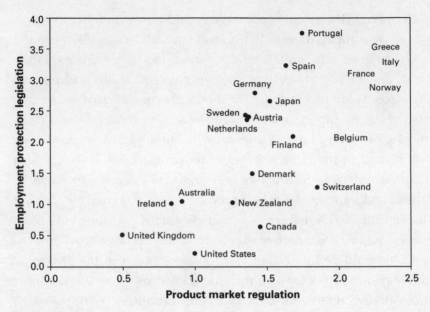

Figure 6.1
Product market regulation and employment protection legislation. Source: G. Nicoletti, S. Scarpetta, and O. Boylaud (1999: Summary indicators of product market regulation with an extension to employment protection legislation. OECD Economics Department, Working paper 226)

tries is run by the unions. The absence of competition produces large rents that are entirely appropriated by the workers. The rents do not show up entirely in high salaries. A large fraction comes in the form of reduced working hours, a relaxed work environment, and other perks. Attacking these unions is not viable. Unions stop the trains, and most governments will give up when faced with a citizens' revolt. An alternative is to allow privately owned companies to run on the same tracks. Although the union of the existing companies will not be happy, it may be possible to build a coalition in favor of this policy: the travelers who have more options, and employees who have new jobs in the new companies.

In summary, lack of competition in the goods and services markets feeds into the problem of labor market lack of flexibility, and the two issues are more interconnected than is often recognized. Reforms of the product markets and of the labor markets would then have the necessary synergies, both economically and politically. A package of labor market and product market reform may be easier to pass politically than two separate parts.

7   Interest Groups against Liberalization

Precisely because European politicians think that they can fix most industrial problems, Europe lacks a strong tradition of independent regulatory agencies. Independent regulators, powerful enough to resist government pressure and impose tough penalties for anti-competitive behavior, are institutions alien to most European governments. Indeed in most countries responsibility for competition policy is still being assigned to government departments and subject to the instructions of politicians. The result is that monopolies and other forms of protection thrive.

Some politicians protect monopolies because they are "captured" by the firms they are supposed to regulate. The theory of regulatory capture, made clear in the early 1970s by George Stigler of the University of Chicago, which won him the Nobel Prize in 1997, holds that public regulators often end up identifying themselves with the firms they are supposed to regulate, so they lose sight of the general welfare of the citizenry they serve. This may happen because of direct bribes or more subtle means like promises of jobs in the industry, or simply persuasion of the regulators by the regulated. In addition, when natural monopolies are state-owned, as is often the case with electricity, gas, and railways, protecting rents means protecting the jobs of government employees. State-owned oil and gas companies, for example, also bring fat revenues to the state treasury, and taxing citizens with high electricity bills is politically less costly than taxing them with income taxes. This is because while an income tax is a direct payment to the government, taxpayers/consumers are usually unaware that they are being taxed through their high electricity bills and believe instead that it is simply becoming more expensive to light their homes. No wonder Europe lacks a serious antitrust culture. As we will discuss shortly, Brussels has changed this, but not without creating other problems.

Why is it so difficult to implement the policies needed to make Europe's markets competitive? Although all consumers stand to benefit from competitive markets for products and services, the broad coalition required to sustain pro-competitive policies never materializes. The political support that could initiate change is simply not there, which is surprising since examples of the benefits of deregulation abound. The taxi market in Ireland is deregulated, and fares there are cheap. For some time after US airlines were deregulated—but European airlines remained regulated—the five-hour flight from New York to Los Angeles cost much less than the half-hour trip from Zurich to Frankfurt. Similar discrepancies are to be found in the price of a coast-to-coast phone call in the United States and that of a domestic long-distance call in France.

Whereas regulation creates unearned rents for overprotected minorities (taxi drivers, notaries, airline pilots, and telecom or electricity workers), deregulation reduces these rents and redistributes them to the general public. Because overprotected minorities enjoy privileged access to politicians, it is no surprise that deregulation incites so much fierce opposition. Low-cost airlines are the main victory of European consumers. This is surprisingly an area where Europe seems to have moved ahead of the United States. But not surprisingly as we discuss below, Europe's major low-cost airline, Ryanair, came under government attack. Under pressure from expensive government-owned airlines, the European Commission recently came very close to causing its ruin.

Is there a way to weaken industry opposition? What if a government, instead of fighting one industry at a time, unleashed an economic Big Bang and liberalized markets all at once? Do we have
examples of successful Big Bang strategies? Here is one. An all or
nothing strategy was adopted by the US Pentagon in the 1980s to
close underutilized military bases. Since 1945 there had not been a
single base closure. Although the Pentagon had in the past desired
to close a good many bases and to use the money elsewhere, no
measure could be passed through the US Congress because military
bases qualify as "pork"—localized public spending programs that
are "gifts" to constituents who help members of Congress get
reelected. Members of Congress hardly ever vote against the pork
in colleagues' districts. Nevertheless, in the government's down-
sizing climate of the 1980s, the plan to close a number of bases
passed by an overwhelming majority. Once the congressional lead-
ership agreed to present a single list of bases to be closed, the list
could only be voted up or down, without any possibility of amend-
ments. So good sense trumped pork.

The citizenry of Europe could benefit from similar strategies. In
the case of electricity, consumer gains from lower prices throughout the economy would more than compensate them for the loss
of rents in their own firms. A Big Bang overhaul could make
deregulation politically easier to enact. Opposition of vested interests could be defused by deregulating the entire economy, and not
select industries one by one. The key to eliminating inefficient,
unproductive subsidies to minorities is to implement tax reductions
for all.

Europe has tried to handle the competition problem by
shifting responsibility for industrial policy away from national
politicians to Brussels. This has met with some success, for three
reasons. First, competition is one of only two policy areas where
the European institutions have executive powers—the other is
monetary policy through the European Central Bank. The decisions

adopted by the Commission have immediate force and, unlike all other decisions, do not require further approval by national governments. Second, it is more difficult to capture or bribe the European Commission than a local politician. Third, Brussels has typically taken the Big Bang approach.

Here are the few success stories. Up to the mid-1990s Italy maintained a large, inefficient state-owned steel industry. The power of unions prevented the government from closing down the industry, which was kept alive thanks to a continuous flow of subsidies. When Brussels made those subsidies illegal, the industry was privatized and the sector opened up to competition. But why did Italy accept the discipline imposed by Brussels? The formal answer is that subsidies are prohibited by the European treaties. The real answer is that Brussels was forcing subsidies out throughout Europe. German savings banks, which enjoyed a government guarantee on their balance sheet, were also forced to give up subsidies. Left to themselves, the Italian government would continue to own steel companies and the German regional banks would continue to enjoy the privilege of a government guarantee. Brussels was able to win both battles by fighting them together. This way it created two natural allies, the German steel industry and Italian banks.

France decided to permit a mild opening of its domestic electricity market the day before the start of formal proceedings against Paris at the European Court of Justice for infringement of an EU directive. Why was the Court of Justice a credible threat? Mainly because other firms in France clearly perceived the cost of challenging the Court's authority. French banks understood that a weakened Court might be unable to resist the pressure of the German government and end up ruling in favor of the German request to lift the prohibition on state guarantees to savings banks. Thus French banks became an important—and unusual—ally of Brussels. By reaching across countries and playing one interest group against another, the Commission is often able to break up deadlocks. This would be much more difficult to achieve at the national level.

Competition policy and the implementation of rules that forbid state aid are, without doubt, the area where Europe has been successful. Particularly since 1999, under Commissioner Mario Monti, Brussels has shown enhanced activism, particularly in attacking cartels (see table 7.1). But precisely because Brussels has made so much progress, governments are striking back. As we already noted, Gunter Verheugen, the new commissioner for industry and vice president of the Barroso Commission, never stops repeating that in the case of "European champions," state aid and antitrust rules should be applied with caution.

But even with European competition policy, Brussels sometimes cannot resist the temptation to overregulate and becomes excessive zealous. Instead of limiting itself to promoting competition and fighting subsidies, occasionally it overreaches. A prominent example has been the ruling against Ryanair in February 2004.

Ryanair has brought cheap fares in a European travel market that not long ago was prohibitively expensive, and it has been a factor in increasing competition in the airline industry, forcing other carriers to reduce fares. Brussels fined Ryanair for having entered into an agreement with Charleroi airport in Belgium. Charleroi in fact was only a small dusty airport with less than 200,000 passengers yearly passing through. Ryanair proposed a tempting deal: the

Table 7.1
Total cartel fines and decisions

	Cartel fines (€ mil)	Number of cartel decisions
1988–1991	60	4
1992–1995	393	11
1996–1999	552	8
2000–2003	3320	26

Source: *Competition Policy International* 1:1 (2005), p. 69.

airport forgoes its landing fees, and in exchange Ryanair flies in two million people a year. The deal was signed and almost everyone was happy: passengers could fly cheaply, the airport rents flourished as shops increased along with the number of passengers, and the local community secured airport jobs. The unhappy were, of course, the big airlines that charge ten times as much as Ryanair and were losing business. Because Charleroi is state-owned, however, in the eyes of the European Commission, forgoing landing fees was tantamount to giving Ryanair state aid. (The presumption here is that the lost revenue must be at the expense of Belgian taxpayers.) So the Commission asked Ryanair to pay back most of the forgone fees, and then announced that it would review the airline's terms of operation at other European airports as well. This was a blow to Ryanair, a big gift to the government-owned airlines such as Alitalia and Air France, and an unexpected gift to those politicians who are just waiting for an occasion to prevent Brussels from interfering with the firms they like to protect. Brussels vetoed the Ryanair deal; since then the Italian government has poured aid into Alitalia to postpone the bankruptcy of this troubled company.

Obviously without public scrutiny of state aid, the state could show favoritism. Or, put differently, how does one distinguish among cases? Our answer is that there should be implicit in government policy the presumption that state aid to any industry or specific company is prohibited. This simple principle should generally guide Brussels' decisions, and only in very special cases should exceptions be made. Ryanair could have been one of the exceptional cases. Alternatively, Brussels could have resolved the state aid problem by instructing the airport to privatize. Once private, Charleroi could sign any agreement it wished with Ryanair or with any other airline. But here we hit a soft spot: European treaties protect competition, but they are neutral vis-à-vis state ownership of companies. The European Union cannot force a member state to privatize; it can only force a state-owned company to be run as if it is a private corporation.

Another story of misguided zeal and pursuit of dubious economic rents is that of the merger cases. Over the past few years the European Court of Justice (to which private parties can appeal decisions made by the Commission) voided a number of decisions in which the Commission had vetoed a corporate merger.

The Court's rulings against Brussels were scathing in their criticism of the Commission's appreciation of the facts. In the Schneider/Legrand steel merger case, it cited "several obvious errors, omissions and contradictions in the Commission's economic reasoning" as well as a "procedural irregularity which constitutes an infringement of defense rights." Similar devastating criticism was raised in the reinstatements of the Tetra Laval and the Airtours/First Choice mergers.

Although the regulations of state aid and of private mergers are separate issues, Brussels' loss of reputation on one battlefield can undermine its position in the battlefield of state aid as well. This is no time for the Commission to lose battles. France, as discussed above, was allowed to return to old policies of bailing out unprofitable private companies on the verge of collapse with taxpayers' money. The Commission's record needs to be consistent if it wishes to win these battles.

Following the setbacks, the Commission has reviewed its procedures in the analysis of mergers. An independent office, headed by an outside economist, was created to evaluate each case. Separated from the Brussels bureaucracy, this office should significantly reduce the risk of the Commission being caught off balance by the Court of Justice. The new Commissioner, Neelie Kroes, has announced a change in focus of competition policy, a new way of thinking that was actually started at the end of the Monti period to deal with the defeats at Court in mergers and antitrust decisions. "The ultimate aim is to protect the consumer. I like vigorous competition by major companies, and I don't care if the competitors are hurt, as long as ultimately the beneficiary is the consumer," Kroes said. One important innovation, in contrast to the Monti era, is that large companies accused of abusing their market position are able to escape punishment if they can demonstrate that their aggressive behavior has benefited consumers in producing market efficiencies, for example, through improved product quality or lower prices, quite independently of the effects on their competitors. These changes have aligned EU antitrust policies with those of the United States, where something similar occurred in the General Electric–Honeywell and Microsoft proposed mergers—the first being a merger approved by the US Department of Justice but vetoed by the European Commission. Recently the European Court of Justice approved the Commission's decision.

A telling weakness in the European approach to fighting cartels is the inability to impose criminal sanctions for cartel behavior. A few years ago a US deputy attorney general related what a senior executive once told him: "As long as you are only talking about money, my company can take care of me, but once you begin talking about taking away my liberty, there is nothing the company can do for me." In the United States, and Canada, individuals engaged in cartels can be prosecuted and sent to jail. In Europe, criminal sanctions for cartel behavior are allowed only in a few countries— Austria, France, Germany, Ireland, and the United Kingdom—but even in this group of countries cartels are typically pursued as civil and not criminal matters.

Finally there is the issue of the Commission's role as prosecutor and judge. In the case of mergers the Commission can open a case against a proposed merger and then decide on it. The parties involved can appeal to the European Court of Justice, but this takes time and a reversal of the Commission's decision typically produces no more than a moral victory to one of the parties. The time of the merger may have come and gone, as in the Airtours/First Choice decision. Division of responsibility between prosecutor and judge is a critical constitutional guarantee for private litigation. One possibility would imply complete separation of competition policy from the Commission, through the creation of an independent European Antitrust authority. A milder solution would be to establish an administrative panel that would make a public recommendation on merger decisions to the entire Commission. This would separate the internal team of investigators and prosecutors from the judges or decision-makers. The commissioners could still overturn the panel's recommendation but not without a good reason.

8 The Judicial System and the Cost of Doing Business

A market economy needs two things in the realm of law in order to function well: first, a judicial system that facilitates transactions of contracts and protects the parties involved, and second, a regulatory environment that achieves the desired goals (ensuring safety, protecting consumers, avoiding negative externalities) without creating unnecessary costs of opening and operating businesses. In all Europe, Italy has the most inefficient and ineffective judicial system, and France is not far behind.

A key ingredient for the functioning of markets (including financial markets) is the enforceability of contracts, which constitutes the trust that the parties have in the speedy application of rules of law. A contract is meaningless without a mechanism of enforcement. Developing countries lag behind in the application of rules of law and contract enforcement, and that this is a major obstacle to a fast catch-up with industrial countries. Among OECD countries there are very large differences in how the judicial systems work and how efficient they are in enforcing contracts. Andrei Shleifer of Harvard University and his collaborators have provided us with very interesting data on the speed with which judicial systems throughout the world enforce certain contracts.

Financial contracts that allow divestiture of risk are particularly important for a market economy. The data in table 8.1 are for two

Table 8.1
Efficiency of the judicial system

| | Eviction of a tenant | | Collection of a check | |
Country	Total duration (days) of judicial procedure	Duration of enforcement in days from issue of judgment to moment owner repossesses property	Total duration (days) of judicial procedure	Days from issue of judgment to moment owner repossesses property
United States	49	10	54	14
Canada	43	17	421	150
Great Britain	115	28	101	14
Ireland	121	50	130	60
France	226	135	181	90
Italy	630	180	645	230
Portugal	330	30		
Greece	247	180	315	90
Holland	52	28	39	15
Spain	183	68	147	29
Belgium	120	57	120	100
Germany	331	111	154	64
Austria	547	180	434	150
Switzerland	266	70	224	90
Japan	363	10	60	10
Denmark	225	25	83	28
Sweden	160	19	190	19
Finland	120	35	240	60

Source: S. Djankov, R. La Porta, F. de Silanes, and A. Shleifer (2003: Courts. *Quarterly Journal of Economic*, May).

typical procedures: collection of funds on a bounced check and eviction of a tenant who refuses to pay rent. Interestingly it takes seven weeks in the United States to collect money on a check or to evict a tenant: five weeks to get a ruling by a court, and two weeks to get the ruling enforced. In Italy, in contrast, it takes more than one year to get a court decision and almost another year to get the ruling enforced. France does slightly better: three months to get a court decision and another three months to get the ruling enforced. In the

Netherlands, however, the time periods are close to those in the United States, and in Sweden they are not as good but much better than in France and Italy. A well-functioning legal system is one of the reasons why Nordic countries in recent years have been able to combine sustained growth despite high taxes.

The effects of an inefficient judiciary are aggravated by a legal profession that remains closed and uncompetitive. Table 8.2 shows the legal expenses required to write a mortgage contract as a fraction of the value of the house being mortgaged. Legal fees at closing can be as high as 20 percent of the mortgage in Italy.

In Germany, because it takes many years for a bank to acquire the title of a house after a borrower has stopped paying the mortgage, banks ask for sizable downpayments. The outcome, as shown in table 8.3, is that less than 10 percent of Germans under 30 own their homes, as opposed to 52 percent in the United Kingdom.

Table 8.2
Cost of legal services

Country	Legal expenses as percentage of mortgage
United States	
Denmark	3–4
Great Britain	4.75
Germany	6
Ireland	10
Portugal	10–20
France	12–18
Holland	11
Spain	5–15
Belgium	16–23
Greece	16
Italy	18–20

Source: M. Bianco, T. Jappelli, and M. Pagano (2005: Courts and banks: Effects of Judicial costs on credit market performance. *Journal of Money Credit and Banking*, April).

Table 8.3
Housing finance and homeownership

	Homeownership by age bracket			Downpayment ratio
	<30	30–39	All	
Australia	30	65	65	23
Austria	21	49	50	33
Belgium	29	62	67	27
Canada	32	65	64	23
Finland	43	76	78	18
France	17	49	56	20
Germany	9.4	29	36	30
Italy	33	48	62	45
Luxembourg	38	55	68	40
Holland	26	56	46	25
Spain	43	66	73	27
Sweden	28	60	58	13
United Kingdom	52	71	66	12
United States	28	58	63	17

Source: Chiuri and Jappelli (2003: Financial market imperfections and home ownership: A comparative study. *European Economic Review*, October).
Note: The downpayment ratio is the average over 1970 to 1995.

The economic consequences of poorly functioning real estate markets can be significant, in particular, for population mobility in regard to labor market flexibility and for population growth in regard to fertility decisions.

The critical consequence of poorly functioning courts is a restriction in the scope of market exchange. When one is not sure whether or not to trust the other party and cannot trust the courts, there is a reluctance to enter into a transaction. Likewise, when a firm is not certain that payment for a delivery to another firm can be enforced, it may hold goods until the cash is on the table, creating delays and inefficiency in economic transactions. Firms also may engage in transactions only with a limited number of other firms, which can restrict the scope of diversification in markets.

Other costs may be indirect and wider in their consequence if ruling against an infraction of the law is slow: those whose moral standards are not high, knowing that courts can take close to forever, could carelessly break contracts. The cost to society is that people will trust one another less, creating more impediments to market exchange. Commerce then is restricted to individuals who know one another, and in the extreme, the impersonality of market transactions disappears.

In Italy legislators have attempted to compensate for slow law enforcement by imposing huge penalties for certain crimes. This has not worked well, however, because the penalties are irregularly enforced, and often the extremely high penalty (jail time) is for a relatively small crime (bouncing a check). The reasoning apparently is, as we saw above, that collecting funds on a bounced check is a very lengthy process. Knowing that in the end one can pay the check to avoid jail, a two-year delay may mean a lot to a cash-strapped perpetrator, but this is no way for a firm to run business transactions.

Where do the differences in the effectiveness of courts come from? We should immediately dispel the typical knee jerk reaction: European countries where the legal systems work better are those with more public money spent on the judiciary. This is simply not true. The data show that variation in public spending as a fraction of GDP is not correlated with the efficiency of the justice system, as measured by indicators like those of table 8.1. So where does the difference come from?

One interesting interpretation is put forward by Andrei Shleifer and Edward Glaeser of Harvard. They observed a correlation between a country's legal system and countries conquered by Napoleon whose legal systems he shaped. These countries tend to have very formalized legal procedures with limited autonomy of judges. Shleifer and Glaeser suggest that transformation of the courts was the result of mistrust, on the part of Napoleon and his revolutionary cohorts of French judges. To limit the discretion of judges, elaborate procedures were adopted. This created the civil code, which is the basis of law practiced in continental Europe. In Great Britain and in the United States, in contrast, judges were trusted and thus allowed to exercise discretion: the less elaborate judicial system is based on common law. Over time, however, the more formal judicial procedures have proved to be more inefficient. Rather than offering more protection to the plaintiffs, they make it possible for judges and bureaucrats to justify their inefficiencies by appealing to formal procedure.

A legal system's inefficiency, makes prosecuting corrupt bureaucrats very difficult. As a result, between individuals and firms and the public administration and regulators, there is lack of confidence in lengthy formal procedures. Because neither the honesty of public servants nor the enforcement mechanism can be trusted, more and more stringent and formal regulations are often substituted, with generally disastrous effects. Corruption does not get reduced and unnecessary costs are created for doing business. It is more or less a vicious circle: the more complicated the regulations get, the more difficult it is to enforce them and the easier it is to cheat. In southern Italy there is a saying *Fatta la legge trovato l' inganno*, which means "as soon as a law is passed we unearth a loophole." An even more cynical suggestion is that complicated regulations create incentives for corrupt bureaucrats to extract rents from individuals in order to allow them to evade them. This may be why regulators favor complicated rules: they facilitate corruption.

As in the case of judicial efficiency, there is wide variation within OECD countries in the cost of doing business. Data collected, once again by Shleifer and collaborators are shown in table 8.4. They give the cost in terms of time as well as the funds necessary to open a business in different countries. Acquiring the necessary permits to open a business takes, on average, 62 working days in Italy, and requires submitting 16 different documents, for a total cost of about US$5,000. In France it takes 53 days, 15 documents, and about US$4,000, and in Germany 42 days, 10 documents, and US$4,000.

Table 8.4
Time and costs regarded to open a business

Country	Number of procedures required to open a business	Time required to complete the procedures (days)	Cost of completing the required procedures
United States	4	4	166.5
Canada	2	2	396.2
Great Britain	5	4	381.4
Ireland	3	16	3,503.7
Finland	5	24	296.8
France	15	53	3,693.0
Italy	16	62	5,012.1
Portugal	12	76	3,370.0
Greece	15	36	10,218.7
Holland	8	31	5,303.2
Spain	11	82	3,731.8
Belgium	8	33	2,736.7
Germany	10	45	3,998.0
Austria	9	41	7,851.4
Switzerland	7	16	5,223.6
Japan	11	26	3,042.9
Denmark	3	3	2,857.3
Sweden	6	13	664.0

Source: Djankov, La Porta, de Silanes, and Shleifer (2003).
Note: The last column is computed by the authors by multiplying the value provided by Djankov et al. of the cost in term of share of per capita income by the per capita income in dollars for each country for 2004.

In the United States the number of required papers is 4, and it takes 4 days to process them at a cost of $166. Once again the Nordic countries, with the lowest level of corruption, fare well on this score. In Sweden, for instance, it takes 6 days and US$664; in Denmark 3 days but almost US$3,000. Recently an Italian film director made a hilarious movie about the tortuous experience of a young entrepreneur dealing with the local bureaucracy in trying to open a dance club in a small Italian town.

Not surprisingly, there are very few new firms created in countries like Italy and France relative to the United States. Also not surprisingly, the excessive costs and regulations create incentives for bribing inspectors and violating the law, or for depending on family connections. Potentially large distortions are inevitable, since the firms created are not the most efficient but the best connected.

In summary, market economies depend on two critical public goods: a well-functioning justice system and good regulation of firms. Provision of these two public goods, together with a third one, law and order, constitutes the most important role of a government. Unlike other types of services, it is difficult for any institution other than government to provide all three. For instance, private provision of education is possible, but private justice, such as arbitration by a third party, cannot easily replace an entire legal system. European governments that fall behind in the provision of these public goods need to focus on them rather than on large investments in faster trains, bigger airports, larger convention centers, and more spectacular bridges, not to mention subsidies to national champions.

9   Conflicts of Interest in Financial Markets

The stock market bubble of the late 1990s fooled many investors. Many people were encouraged to think that stocks could yield 20 percent returns year after year. The bubble also fooled boardrooms, inducing some CEOs to think that they could get away with opaque derivative contracts to transfer cash from their companies to their pockets. Horror stories of cheated investors surfaced on both sides of the Atlantic: Enron, Tyco, and WorldCom in the United States; Parmalat in Italy; Royal Ahold in Holland. In Germany, where supervisory boards of firms are a peculiar mix of shareholder representatives and unions that share the responsibility for running a company, all sorts of inappropriate practices occurred (more on these peculiar institutions later). Underlying some of these scandals were conflicts of interest that were encouraged by inappropriate practices of financial firms and their overseers. This happened throughout Europe and in the United States, notably in the New York Stock Exchange.

What was different on the two sides of the Atlantic was the response to the scandals. The US Congress acted swiftly to amend corporate law, and the New York Stock Exchange (NYSE) removed its chairman, Richard Grasso, and changed its governance rules. In Europe the conflicts of interest, both within the large universal banks and between the banks and their regulators, and sometimes within the same regulatory agencies, have remained unchanged—

and so have the risks investors keep facing. These conflicts and their costs are the subject of this chapter. Once again, it is instructive to start with the United States.

There is an obvious connection between the Enron, Tyco, and WorldCom scandals and what was revealed about the way the NYSE used to work when its chairman got engulfed in the outrage over his huge severance pay. The entire fiasco on the part of the NYSE board of directors can be traced to the way boards are frequently packed with the chairman's friends and associates, who are unlikely to ask tough questions or to be picky when it comes to decide how much the CEO should be paid. The NYSE is the regulator of the stock market, but its board members were being drawn from the very market it regulated, bringing along serious conflicts of interest. Over the years the directors from some of the largest New York brokerage firms, which are regulated by the exchange, came to dominate the board. When the chairman demanded a severance package that amounted to $139.5 million in deferred pay and retirement benefits, they went along, leaving the public with the impression that Grasso, one of their own, was privy to their abuses of privilege. To remove this conflict of interest—while maintaining the exchange as a self-regulated entity—the new chairman, John Reed, acted to enhance its independence. Board members can no longer be brokers, or affiliated with one of the firms listed on the exchange. Brokers and listed firms are now limited to an advisory role.

Enron declared bankruptcy in February 2002. By July of the same year the US Congress had passed the Sarbanes-Oxley Act. Combined, the new law, and the new stock exchange rules, have increased the independence of company directors and reduced conflicts of interest. A majority of board members of listed companies now must be independent. Also audit and compensation committees must consist entirely of independent directors; company auditors cannot provide consulting services for the company. Another provision, and by far the most critical, is that board members individually sign the accounts of the firm. This way they become responsible if anything goes wrong. Similar rules were introduced in the United Kingdom, with a new code of corporate governance.

The Sarbanes-Oxley provisions are far from perfect, and several economists have justly criticized them. They questioned whether the company founders or original financiers ever intended such restrictions to be placed on their companies or boards. The new law, they argued, overrides agreements entered into voluntarily by these initial investors. In addition it increases legal costs, wastes board time, and deters new companies from going public. These objections raise an important issue that laws passed hurriedly to "fix" a problem, such as the Enron crisis, are often not well thought out. On the contrary, they reduce efficiency and burden the very sectors they seek to protect. This law can, and should, be improved. But at least the speed with which the US Congress responded to the scandals has worked to restore the confidence of investors, particularly small investors. Nevertheless, capitalist markets are not perfect, and neither does state intervention always correct misconduct and fraud.

It took two years for the Italian Parliament to respond to the Cirio and Parmalat scandals, and the law that was finally passed has at least as many shortcomings as the Sarbanes-Oxley Act. In Italy, investments have plummeted as investors became convinced that the Italian Parliament was siding with the wrongdoers and not with the small shareholders.

The conflicts of interest that plague European financial markets have three main causes. The first, as we mentioned before, is the peculiar governance structure of German firms. German private corporations (GmbHs) with more than 500 employees, and all listed companies, have two boards: a supervisory board and a management board. On the supervisory board one-half (in large companies) or one-third (in smaller companies) of all the seats are reserved for union representatives. Day to day operations are run by the management board (with no unions' representatives), but the members of the management board are appointed by the supervisory board, which also sets their salaries and makes all strategic decisions. This peculiar arrangement does not simply redistribute the firm's surplus away from shareholders and toward workers, which alone can result in less investment. The presence of unions on the supervisory board affects the firm's strategic decisions. Firms with a supervisory board are slower to restructure and adjust to change by making employment or wage cuts. This creates obstacles to the creative destruction, which, as we discussed in chapter 5, is critical for growth. The European Commission tried to solve the problem by allowing EU-based firms to incorporate under EU legislation rather than national legislation. By choosing to do so, German companies could eliminate their supervisory boards and replace them with normal boards. So far, however, very few German firms have taken advantage of this option.

A second type of conflict of interest is one that exists within universal banks. An overwhelming majority of mutual funds in continental Europe are owned by banks. Independent companies, such as Fidelity in the United States, are the exception in Europe. A bank that manages a mutual fund also underwrites the securities issued by a client. It has all sorts of perverse incentives to boost demand by stuffing its own mutual funds with those securities. If it fears that a firm is not able to repay a loan, it may try to convince the firm to issue a corporate bond. It can then place the bond in the portfolio of its funds and transfer the risk away from the balance sheet. It can also ask its mutual funds to use the bank as a broker, even if its fees are higher than elsewhere, and in this way boost the bank's profits at the expense of investors. This is what clearly emerged in the aftermath of the bankruptcies of Cirio and Parmalat, two Italian companies. In both cases the banks came out virtually unscathed, and the losses were borne disproportionately by small investors. Something similar happened with Argentinean bonds. The banks owned no defaulted bonds; they had all been placed in the portfolios of their clients. Why would anybody invest in these mutual funds? Why can't European households move all their savings to Fidelity? The answer is that the market is dominated by a small cartel of large banks. These banks do not compete with one another, and they make sure that the regulators keep Fidelity at a distance. The outcome is apparent in table 9.1, which shows the top ten asset management companies in Italy and Spain. In Italy asset management is entirely controlled by domestic banks; in Spain only one foreign bank, Barclays, has been able to gain entry into the banking sector.

A third type of conflict of interest has to do with the misguided behavior of regulators. Bank supervision in continental Europe is typically under the aegis of national central banks. When confronted with the bankruptcy of a large firm the central bank has to choose between two strategies: let the commercial banks suffer the loss in their loan books, or look the other way as the banks—which thanks to

Table 9.1
Top ten asset managers in Spain and Italy, 2004

Italy	Spain
SanPaolo	Santander
Unicredit	BBVA
Intesa	La Caixa
Assicurazioni Generali	Caja Madrid
MPS	Ahorro Corporación
Capitalia	Banco Popular
RAS	Bankinter
Arca	Banco Sabadell
Popolare Verona	Barclays
BNL	Ibercaja

their relationship with the firm often learn about the possibility of a bankruptcy ahead of time—transfer the losses onto small investors. The behavior of the Bank of Italy in the Cirio bankruptcy is a good example of this strategy. In the months that preceded the bankruptcy a large Italian bank placed newly issued Cirio bonds in the portfolios of its clients, using the proceeds to repay the loans it had extended to Cirio. The same happened a few years later in the Parmalat scandal. In neither case did the Bank of Italy object.

Why don't European parliaments intervene and change the law to make it more difficult for banks to mistreat their customers? Again, we turn to Italy for an interesting case study. After the Cirio and Parmalat scandals the Italian Parliament started to discuss a law that would protect investors and transfer some regulatory functions away from the central bank. Immediately a strong lobby formed and blocked any interference with the banks and the central bank. The law bounced to and fro, and after two years a milder version was approved—and only after the judiciary charged a few bankers with criminal misconduct, and the governor of the central bank was himself under judicial scrutiny.

The conflict of interest problems can be traced to the fact that the national central banks of the euro area, and their governors, in particular, never accepted the simple idea that the creation of a monetary union and a European Central Bank would inevitably reduce their power. Having lost the ability to set monetary policy, they retreated into banking supervision and regulation, trying to justify through these activities their existence and the overblown size of their staff.

One of the most serious problems is a bias against the cross-border consolidation of European banks, an important development if the eurozone is to become a truly integrated financial area. When a home bank is purchased by a bank from another EU country, responsibility for supervising this bank is transferred to the authorities of the buying country and the home central bank loses part of its business. However in most countries, France, Portugal, Spain, Holland, and Italy among them, the central bank is responsible for banking regulation and supervision, and thus has a de facto veto power over mergers. The hostility of central banks is the main reason why cross-border consolidation is not happening.

A recent example that borders on the ridiculous occurred when a large Dutch bank sought to buy a mid-sized Italian bank. Worried about the prospect of losing a "client," the governor of the Bank of Italy, Antonio Fazio, asked a friend who runs a small provincial bank in northern Italy to organize a counterbid. The friend's bank was small and not particularly sound: even the officials in charge of supervision within the Bank of Italy were astounded. But this did not stop the governor, who authorized the counterbid. Eventually the Italian judiciary stepped in and charged Fazio with insider trading and with transgression of power. The Italian bid was ended, and the governor was forced to resign—but by the judges and not by any financial regulator.

Fortunately, not all eurozone central banks carry on this way. In Germany, after the introduction of the euro, the Bundesbank dramatically cut its staff. Also banking supervision in Germany is assigned to an independent entity. In 2005, when an Italian bank bought the second largest German bank, the Bundesbank did not intervene.

What are some national central banks trying to defend? First, as mentioned above, their power has been compromised by the creation of the ECB. Next is the matter of parting with rich salaries in reducing their staffs. Across Europe per capita spending by the central banks is strikingly different. Total staff costs at the Banque de France and the Banca d'Italia alone are almost as high as for the entire Federal Reserve System (US$1.4 billion in France, US$1.2 billion in Italy, as compared to $1.6 in the United States—an area several times the sizes of France and Italy. The data are for 2004.). The euro system costs every EU citizen $15, the Federal Reserve $5, and the Bank of England (which admittedly is not responsible for banking supervision) US$3. New Zealand, the Czech Republic and Canada, each are less than US$3 per person. France costs US$23 per person, Italy US$21, Austria US$25, and Greece US$30, and this after each of these national central banks has seen its responsibility for running monetary policy transferred to the ECB.

Some central banks may also be trying to justify the salaries of their governors. The governor of the Bank of Italy earns more than €600,000 a year (the exact figure is not disclosed), which is almost three times as much as his colleague in Finland, twice as much as the president of the New York Fed, and €200,000 more than his boss in Frankfurt, the president of the ECB. Alan Greenspan took home US$172,000—before taxes, which is probably far too low. (The data in table 9.2, the most up-to-date that we could find, refer to 2003.)

What hurts competition in banking is not concentration per se (which allows banks to exploit scale economies) but restrictions on the entry of new banks in the market. Being open to new entry is the most important competitive pressure. The United States likewise used to have an old-fashioned, uncompetitive, and inefficient banking industry. But with the repeal of interstate banking restrictions through the 1994 Riegle-Neal Act, banking was transformed. The opening up of a coast-to-coast market allowed Nationsbank (later Bank of America) to exploit huge economies of scale, while at the same time entering sleepy, protected local markets and turning them around to the benefit of their consumers.

European central banks are right when they promote consolidation among banks, but they are wrong when they force the process to happen within the domestic borders. By doing this, they only hurt consumers. It should be no surprise that two of the most dynamic European banks, Santander and Bilbao of Spain, operate in the only European country that opened up its banking market years ago.

Table 9.2
Salaries of central bank governors

Bank governor	Salary (in US$)
Joseph Yam (Hong Kong)	1,120,000
Antonio Fazio (Bank of Italy)	>600,000[a]
Malcolm Knight (BIS)	450,000
Nout Wellink (Netherlands)	440,000
Jean Pierre Roth (Swiss National Bank)	429,000
Wim Duisenberg (ECB)	417,000
Mervyn King (Bank of England)	411,160
Ian Macfarlane (Australia)	325,123
John Hurley (Ireland)	315,000
Bill McDonough (New York Fed)	315,000
Toshihiko Fukui (Bank of Japan)	276,076
Alan Bollard (New Zealand)	255,672
Bodil Nyboe Andersen (Denmark)	253,000
Klaus Liebscher (Austria)	247,150
Lars Heikenstein (Sweden)	241,000
Matti Vanhala (Finland)	233,000
Alan Greenspan (Federal Reserve)	172,000
Zdenek Tuma (Czech National Bank)	110,000

Source: CentralBankNet.com.
Note: Data refer to 2003.
a. Exact amount is not disclosed.

The euro has induced European firms to tap markets issuing securities, corporate bonds in particular. But, surprisingly, it is US banks that help European firms issue corporate bonds (as shown in table 9.3). US banks have been fast to transfer to Europe the experience they have acquired in the US domestic market. Capital market services involve large economies of scale—in company research and in the distribution of the bonds to large institutional investors. These services do not call for strong local presence and are typically demanded by a few large firms with easy access to international banks. Small European banks suffer a comparative disadvantage: a lack of strong client relationships with European firms that have started issuing bonds.

Table 9.3
Financial markets tapped by European firms as percentage of all corporate bond issues in euro area

	1995	2000
Bank of same nationality as the issuing firm	80	37
Bank of another euro area country	16	15
US bank	4	48

However, in the European banking industry there are a few winners. The few success stories have mostly happened in Germany and Holland. In 1997, before the euro was introduced, there was only one eurozone institution among the largest European asset managers, the French insurance company AXA. Today there are four and the three newcomers are two from Germany, one from the Netherlands.

From the recent European banking scandals we learn how powerful and well-organized interest groups can collude to defend their privileges. Rather than risk financing new business ideas, bankers run a comfortable life issuing loans to existing firms with good collateral assets. Whenever they make a mistake even in this "plain vanilla" business, they promptly transfer the losses onto their consumers. Parliaments should protect the public, but in an environment unduly influenced by the banking lobbysts, how are innovation and productivity to thrive?

10   A United Europe?

Many European politicians believe that the answer to European decline is the European Union. A United Europe would give economic and political strength to the region and would set it as an economic and political balance to the United States. However, is a union of ailing European countries the solution? It may well be that European Union enthusiasts are way too optimistic about the benefits and the realistic prospects of a United Europe. On the other hand, the so-called eurosceptics may simply want to isolate themselves from the pressures to reform that come from Brussels.

Whether European integration can achieve its objective depends on how it is accomplished. For example, union means coordination of policies. But coordination is not the answer in many areas: too much of it, or in the wrong direction, may precipitate rather than avert a decline.

The whole process of European integration is hard to explain to most people. Steps forward on the United Europe project—such as the introduction of the euro in 1998 or the Single Market project in 1985—have often been followed by long periods of inactivity on the United Europe project. At the time of this writing (early 2006), the rejection of the proposed constitution for Europe by France and the Netherlands has created an especially critical impasse.

This chapter is based on A. Alesina and R. Perotti, 2004, The European Union: A politically incorrect view, *Journal of Economic Perspectives* (Fall), pp. 27–48.

The accepted wisdom in Europe is that the rejection of the proposed constitution is a serious setback. However, this development may be paradoxically a healthy one: it has brought out the differences of opinion between European citizens and their leaders.

Traditionally the cleavage between those involved in building European integration was attributed to clashes between the so-called intergovernmentalists and the so-called federalists. The former view Europe as a system of economic integration and cooperation among independent governments; the federalists instead imagine a sort of United States of Europe, a true political federation. The former group has traditionally included France and the United Kingdom, the latter group many German politicians, some Italians, some Spaniards, and many smaller countries and especially the so-called Eurocrats composed of the civil servants serving in Brussels with the European Commission. The tension between the two views and the intrinsic difficulties in forming a union of so diverse twenty-five countries have led to a long and tortuous process of institution building. The functioning of the bodies governing Europe is so complex that very few Europeans, let alone Americans, know exactly who does what. In an appendix to this chapter we provide a summary of the functions of the main EU institutions.

The compromises between the federalist and intergovernmentalist positions have led to a complex web of institutions. Some are federalist in nature, like the Commission, and others, intergovernmental in nature, like the European Council of Ministers (see the appendix for details). The attempt to balance the intergovernmentalist and federalist positions has produced an institutional design that lacks clarity. First of all, in the European Union no clear separation of powers exists. For instance, the Commission has both executive and legislative power, but they are shared with the European Council and the European Parliament. Second, the allocation of who does what in

Europe is often more the result of a compromise based on who is more powerful at a meeting rather than on any economic or institutional rationale. The result is that Brussels does too much in some areas (agriculture, social policy, coordination and fine-tuning of fiscal policy) and too little in others (promotion of a true common market in all sectors).

The one thing certain is that Brussels keeps edging into more and more areas. Table 10.1 shows this tendency as measured by the increasing number of legislative acts issued in Brussels. The three forms of EU legislation (regulations, directives, and decisions) have increased from about 2,600 acts in the early 1970s, reaching about 11,400 in the late 1990s—a 500 percent increase. About half of the legislative acts concerned agriculture, a sector that produces about 2 percent of Europe's GDP. Truth be told, this is a little misleading, since most of the legislative provisions in agriculture are for such minutia as the appropriate size of melons, compared with broader coverage of legislation in other areas. Still the fact that in the 1990s the Europe Union could pass several thousand regulations and directives for agriculture is astounding.

Indeed table 10.1 gives credence to arguments of critics of the European Union that there are far too many laws and regulations coming from Brussels. Apparently, for many years, the underlying philosophy in Brussels was that only laws and regulations can ensure good functioning of society, despite ample evidence of the silliness of the regulations. We hope that the current pro-market head of the European Commission, José Manuel Barroso of Portugal, will strike down about one-third of European regulations and directives, as he promised. No doubt Europe will continue to thrive without orders from Brussels and the average European will hardly notice the difference.

So what should the European Union do and not do? It is reasonable to start thinking about the allocation of prerogatives between

Table 10.1
EU legislation (regulations, directives, and decisions) by policy domain

	1971–1975	1976–1980	1981–1985	1986–1990	1991–1995	1996–2000
International trade	864	2,573	2,208	3,416	2,783	2,041
Common market	133	251	184	268	305	529
Money and fiscal	49	69	98	65	100	249
Education, research, culture	15	40	73	104	180	136
Environment	29	61	98	131	197	255
Business relation, sectoral	**1,155**	**3,051**	**5,685**	**7,281**	**7,130**	**5,437**
Agriculture and fishery	980	2,479	5,165	6,880	6,654	4,907
Industry and energy	109	455	408	300	309	370
Transport	66	127	112	101	167	160
Business nonsectoral (compet/subs/ company law)	116	137	256	358	669	1,406
International relations and foreign aid (without international trade)	155	100	162	768	426	501
Citizens and social protection	96	126	263	521	700	860
Total	2,612	6,408	9,027	12,912	12,560	11,414

Shares (% of column)						
International trade	33.1	40.2	24.5	26.5	22.2	17.9
Common market	5.1	3.9	2.0	2.1	2.4	4.6
Money and fiscal	1.9	1.1	1.1	0.5	0.8	2.2
Education, research, culture	0.6	0.6	0.8	0.8	1.4	1.2
Environment	1.1	1.0	1.1	1.0	1.6	2.2
Business relation, sectoral	**42.2**	**47.6**	**63.0**	**56.4**	**56.8**	**47.6**
Agriculture and fishery	37.5	38.7	57.2	53.3	53.0	43.0
Industry and energy	4.2	6.9	4.5	2.3	2.5	3.2
Transport	2.5	2.0	1.2	0.8	1.3	1.4
Business nonsectoral (compet/subs/company law)	4.4	2.1	2.8	2.8	5.3	12.3
International relations and foreign aid (without international trade)	5.9	1.6	1.8	5.9	3.4	4.4
Citizens and social protection	3.7	2.0	2.9	4.0	6.1	7.5
Total	100.0	100.0	100.0	100.0	100.0	100.0

Source: A. Alesina, I. Angeloni, and L. Schucknecht (2005: What does the European Union do? *Public Choice*).
Note: Data include all acts issued in the period, including those no longer in force today.

Brussels and the member states as trade-offs between economies of scale and heterogeneities of preferences. Government activities with relevant to economies of scale, which benefit from being large, could be allocated to Brussels. The obvious example is the single market. Because the benefits of a single market are larger in the larger market, the common market policies clearly belong to Brussels. The same can be said about foreign policy and defense. Some infrastructures also have relevant economies of scale. However, the trade-off in delegating all such activities to Brussels is that national choices over policies will become restricted and diminish national sovereignty. Take the case, at the opposite extreme of the spectrum, of policies about school curricula. Clearly, economies of scale are not at all relevant in this area, but heterogeneity of preferences across countries and even within regions of the same country may be large. Therefore a policy of EU uniformity on school curricula does not make sense.

Many policy areas fall in between the two extremes of common market policies (where economies of scale dominate) and school curricula (where heterogeneity of preferences dominates). So member states have to trade off the benefits of economies of scale versus the costs of uniformity, that is, the cost of not allowing all the different countries to follow their own preferences. Think of fiscal policies, for example. Normalizing certain tax rules is necessary, for instance, to ensure a common financial market. Imposing UK welfare rules on the people of Sweden, who enjoy more generous provisions of welfare, instead does not make sense, nor is it a requirement for a well-functioning common market. Even in the United States, welfare rules vary greatly across the states.

The sharing of responsibilities between Brussels and national governments has often departed from the principles outlined above. A foreign policy at the EU level does not exist. Rather Brussels has been increasingly involved in setting rules about social policies that often infringe on national autonomy in ways that seem unnecessary. As table 10.1 shows, a large increase in the volume of EU legislative acts occurred in the area of citizens' social protection. At the moment the Europe Union is engaged in a heated discussion with the United Kingdom to force it to adopt regulations on mandatory vacations that are uniform to the continental European model. As we showed in chapter 3, different countries have different social equilibria regarding hours worked. Brussels is disregarding this difference in trying to dictate vacation-taking policy.

In addition to intergovernmentalism versus federalism, a second and much more inportant divide has come to dominate the European debate: the dirigiste economic management style of France and the free market, laissez faire style of the United Kingdom. Not surprisingly allied with the first camp is Germany and with the second are Ireland, some northern European countries, and new entrants from the center and eastern parts of Europe. The debate in France leading up to the rejection of the European constitution could not be clearer on this point. Both camps, the "oui" and the "non," justified their positions as a way of preventing France from adopting laissez faire policies characterized as "Anglo-Saxon ultra liberalism," the (in)famous term coined by French President Jacques Chirac.

The French "non" has cleared the table of exotic debates about institutional details and brought into the open what the real issues are. Although France and the United Kingdom are both traditionally intergovernmentalists, they have become leaders of the two opposing sides of Europe, another indication of where the real tension is. The laissez faire approach to Europe views the latter as a common market area in which most, if not all, countries have adopted a common currency, but not much more. The dirigiste approach views Europe as a fortress to be somehow protected from excessive foreign competition by an active public sector that promotes domestic development.

On the question of a common foreign and defense policy the United Kingdom and France are likewise on opposite sides. If Europe is to "balance" (a euphemism for "challenge") the United States, France's hope is to lead Europe's foreign policy out from under NATO's umbrella. The UK view is not necessarily opposed to a European foreign policy, as long as it is viewed in the context of NATO, and therefore it is more favorable to a transatlantic alliance.

In summary, the relevant conflict in Europe is not between federalists and intergovernmentalists. The real cleavage is different. On the one side are the French dirigiste and protectionist economic terms, favoring a foreign policy outside of NATO and outside American influence. On the other is a vision of Europe as a free market within the traditional role of NATO and the transatlantic alliance. To be sure, there are subtleties, for many Europeans believe in markets as well as in a federated Europe.

However, a European Union based on the French vision of the economy does not make sense. It contradicts the very idea behind a European Union, which was to create a very large single market. A single market has indeed been pretty much achieved for the market of goods, but it is far from being reached in the market for services. Today services comprise almost two-thirds of the GDP of European countries, and their future depends on this sector. France's recent positions have severely pushed back attempts by the European Commission to create a true European free market in the service sectors. "Economic patriotism" is a new phrase, but the term patriotism really replaces protectionism in the realm of trade.

The movement of labor forces, especially from the new member states in central and eastern Europe, is a sensitive issue, as we discussed in chapter 2. But protection of a domestic market from competition is a contradictory goal within unions, since mobility of labor is the basis on which unions are founded. Nevertheless, one of the motivations behind the French rejection of the EU constitution was the fear of a rush of cheap labor from the new member states.

A notion that Europe can be open as a well-functioning internal market but closed to trade outside the "fortress" is also problematic for one obvious reason. Large European firms run global operations. A fortress Europe would be subject to trade retaliation. Further, because Europe needs to attract migrant workers, it would end up with borders open to foreign workers but borders closed to the goods they produce. This turn of affairs would run contrary to basic economic principles.

Already Europe is protectionist in some areas. Again, agricultural policy is a case in point. The agricultural sector absorbs almost half of the EU budget but is less than 2 percent of EU GDP. Recall that nearly 50 percent of the EU legislative acts are for agriculture. The chief beneficiary of EU agricultural policy is France, which receives a subsidy of more than €9 billion, or 21 percent of the total (the numbers refer to 2004). Besides not helping to relieve poverty in the developing world, this policy favors rich European farmers and is creating conflicts even within Europe because of the unfair distribution of the subsidies.

Contrary to the accepted wisdom that agricultural policy should protect the small farmer and thus help preserve the culture of small farming communities, large sums of money are going into European agri-business and to people who are well connected. Some examples: Prince Albert II of Monaco receives €300,000 a year for his farm in France, and the Queen of England €546,000 (in 2003). The three largest beneficiaries of agricultural aid in Holland are the large companies Phillip Morris (€1.46 million in 2003), Royal Dutch Shell (€660,000), and Van Drie, an agri-business company (€745,000); the same pattern occurs in Spain. Nestlé in the United

Kingdom received €11.3 million in 2004, Tate & Lyle, Europe's main cane sugar refiner, €127 million. These are the only countries for which we could obtain data. We suspect that similar sizable sums are paid out in France and in Germany. So much for concern for the small European farmer! But even if agricultural subsides could reach the small farmers, the question is Why should they deserve special protection?

In the case of foreign and defense policy, there is the prospect of a European common policy outside of NATO that will challenge US dominance. Such policy is, however, destined to remain a fantasy for several reasons. First of all, European countries cannot agree on what direction to take. The United Kingdom clearly has a separate view from the rest of Western Europe, where divergence is great anyway, as the crisis in former Yugoslavia revealed. At the beginning of that 1995 crisis Germany and France were squarely in opposite camps, because of their past alliances in the region. Today a majority of Europeans claim they want a European foreign policy, but beyond deep anti-Americanism, very little else is there as far as a common foreign policy is concerned. Of course, within the United States there are also sharp differences on foreign policy, and presently there are great differences among Americans about their country's intervention in Iraq. Nevertheless, Americans are willing to allow the president to make foreign policy and generally accept the decisions of the president while he is in office. Europeans are a long way from coming close to this consensus.

Second, Europeans are unable to spend more on defense to reach the military capability of the United States. The US military spending is larger than that of the 25 EU countries combined. Europe spends about 2 percent of GDP on defense and the United States 3.5 percent of GDP. The difference is that in the past the United States was spending up to 6 percent of GDP and thus has accumulated a vast arsenal of weaponry and military technology. The American army is far more advanced than European armies, to the point that, according to military experts, the American army and the European armies have trouble communicating. There is risk, as the American ambassador to NATO, Nicholas Burns, remarked recently, that "Without dramatic action to close the capabilities gap, we face the real prospect of a two-tiered alliance." The alliance "is so unbalanced" he said, "that we may no longer have the ability to fight together in the future." The differences in technology, with the possible exception of the British army, are almost insurmountable. To begin to close the gap, Europeans would have to make a huge investment in military spending, in addition to the close to 50 percent of GDP they already spend as compared to the 30 percent in the United States. It is hard to imagine highly taxed Europeans able to pay any more taxes. A country as rich as Germany is still unable to deliver on schedule more than a third of the troops promised for peacekeeping in Kabul because it must rent Russian or Ukrainian transport planes on the commercial market. One country, which NATO officials refused to identify, discussed moving troops to Kabul by railroad. Yet a European troop transport plane, the A-400 M, a variant of the European-owned Airbus, is stuck in a financing dispute in Germany. Even worse, the plane will take eight to ten years to deliver. Europe spends about $140 billion a year on the military, but on average only about $7,000 per soldier compared with $28,000 per American soldier on research and development.

Third, Europeans are reluctant to use military force, even when there appears to be no alternative, as the crises in former Yugoslavia clearly show. In July 1995 in Srebrenica, the Dutch sent peacekeepers. But what "peace" did they keep? They dropped their guns and watched more than 7,000 Muslim civilians being massacred. No European power stepped up to bomb the Serbian positions. It took the Americans to strategize the bombing, which subdued the Serbs. Richard Holbrooke, the Clinton envoy in Serbia, recounts this experience in the Balkans in his book *How to End a War*. The Dutch government's fear was that the air strikes would endanger its own soldiers in Bosnia. The other Europeans were ready to put the lives of their soldiers ahead of their military duty as well. At the very border of the Union, it was therefore left to Americans, coming from several thousand miles away, to force the issue and militarily intervene. In fact it was precisely because the Europeans had not spent enough on defense that their soldieries were more at risk on the ground than American soldiers. The European aversion to use force has resulted in a lack of a credible threat of military intervention and this circumstance further makes diplomatic pressure less effective.

Nonexistence of a truly European foreign policy has not stopped European rhetoric about it. In the years between 1994 and 1997, at the time of the European failure in Yugoslavia, the European Union adopted 66 common positions on just about every foreign policy issue under the sun and issued 163 declarations in 1998 alone, amounting to one every two days including weekends and holidays. Chris Patten, the British European Commissioner from 1999 to 2004, noted that "they came usually a week or two after they could influence anything."

In summary, a non–laissez faire Europe with domestic markets protected from globalization makes no sense, and a single foreign policy for Europe seems very far from what today is feasible. The way for the European project to move forward therefore lies in the reach of the single market. But here too Brussels cannot impose upon European countries what they do not want. If the French and Germans do not want, say, liberalization of the service sector, Brussels cannot force them to liberalize. Or, if Brussels wants uniform labor standards, it cannot impose upon the United Kingdom the continental Europe type of labor market legislation. In the past the European Commission was often successful in overcoming national opposition and getting its proposals (good or bad) approved. Recent experience shows that national interests easily prevail over EU interests: the Stability and Growth Pact was for all practical purposes dismissed as soon as the French and Germans could not obey its rules; liberalization of the service sector proposed by the Commission was watered down by the European Parliament with the vote of French and German members.

Construction of a united Europe has not been easy. Over and over the European Union has had to abandon misplaced dreams. What is important today is for Europe to focus on reforms in the next decade. Economic reform can be helped by ensuring a common and free market by eliminating all barriers to trade and competition. It is further up to every government body of the European Union to thwart the dirigisme, the empty rhetoric and excessive reliance on coordination of polices imposed from above, that is counterproductive and generates reactions against the Union, even against the good things it does. We take up the issue of this rhetoric in the next chapter.

Appendix: A Brief Summary of EU Institutions[1]

Governance of the European Union was conceived of as comprising three parts, called three pillars. At the heart of the first pillar are the so-called four freedoms of movement: of persons, goods, capital, and services. These freedoms are understood to be accompanied by a single market and competition. Some other issues under this pillar are agriculture, competition, and trade, and (recently added) visa privileges and asylum policies. The second pillar includes Common Security and Foreign Policy (CSFP), and the third pillar, Justice and Home Affairs, now covers mostly police and judicial cooperation in criminal matters.

There is a fundamental difference between the first pillar and the second and third pillars: EU institutions can pass legislation that is

---

1. This appendix is reproduced, with minor changes, from Alesina and Perotti (2004).

directly applicable and has *primacy* over individual members' law for first pillar issues. In contrast, any decision affecting the two other pillars requires unanimity, and must be approved by national parliaments to be applicable in member states. What follows is a brief description of the main roles of each EU institution. The following abbreviations are used: "Council" for Council of the European Union, "Commission" for the Commission of the European Union, "EP" for European Parliament, "DC" for draft constitution, and "QMV" for qualified majority voting.

The European Council

The European Council, which should not be confused with the Council of the European Union to be introduced below, is the forum where the heads of state of the European Union and the president of the Commission meet to discuss general issues. It has no formal decision-making power, yet it is the most influential body. It is here that all the major policy guidelines are set and that all decisions on the big issues are taken. The European Council meets at least every six months, and it makes all decisions unanimously. The presidency rotates every six months among all EU members.

The Council of the European Union

This body has both executive authority, which it has in large part delegated to the Commission, and legislative authority. All regulations and directives (the two most important legislative acts of the EU) must be approved by the Council, either jointly with the EP or after consultation with it. The Council is composed of one representative from each country, usually the national minister in charge of the issue under discussion. Hence, although it is a single institution, the Council has several incarnations. One of the most visible is ECOFIN, the meeting of the finance ministers to discuss, monitor, and coordinate budgetary matters. Overall, the Council meets between eighty and ninety times in a typical year. The Council decides by unanimity in the most sensitive areas (including some first pillar issues), and in most cases by qualified majority voting. The current QMV procedure assigns a certain number of votes to member countries as a function of their population size, but weighted in a way that favors small countries relative to strict proportionality.

The European Commission

The Commission has several roles. Among the most important are:

1. *Right to initiate legislation* The Council and the EP cannot approve any piece of legislation if it has not been proposed by the Commission.

2. *Executive power* The Commission monitors the implementation of the main legislation adopted by the European Union.

3. *Regulatory power* The Commission regulates mostly in the area of public undertakings.

4. *Power of surveillance of European law* The Commission is the guardian of the European treaties. If it detects infringement of a treaty, after an attempt to resolve the matter, it refers it to the European Court of Justice.

5. *"Watchdog" of the Economic and Monetary Union* The Commission monitors compliance with the economic policies agreed on at the beginning of each year, and recommends various types of actions to the Council in case of noncompliance.

The Commission and its President are first nominated and then appointed by member countries after approval by the EP. Currently each country has 1 commissioner.

The European Parliament

The EP is directly elected in all EU member countries for five years and shares the legislative and budgetary authority with the Council.

The Council's opinion prevails in matters of "compulsory spending" (mostly agriculture), while the EP's position prevails on the other matters—yet another example of the system's institutional balance.

The European Court of Justice

The EU Court of Justice can "interpret" EU law and seek its application. Court cases can be initiated both by governments and private citizens who have access through the Court of First Instances. Unlike American practice, its judicial rulings do not have legal stature in the European Union. Still the Court of Justice has acquired considerable stature among the EU bodies. Recently its involvement in competition policy has been widely publicized.

11

The Rhetoric of
Dirigisme and
Coordination

Policy-making within the European Union is torn between the Anglo-French cleavage described in the previous chapter. On the one hand, a united Europe has had a positive impact in deregulation of certain sectors (a topic we discussed in chapter 7), in the introduction of a single currency (a topic we address in chapter 12), and in promoting some fiscal discipline (a topic we tackle in chapter 13). On the other hand, it has been a source of dirigiste rhetoric that has set debates in the wrong direction and confused rather than clarified the issues facing Europe. The European Union has set very complicated procedures, meetings, and periodic reviews that call for the writing of dozens of planning documents and lengthy reviews of these plans. Here we discuss three examples.

The "Lisbon process" has reached an extraordinary status in Europe, so much so that in some circles it appears that the future of Europe depends on implementation of the "Lisbon Agenda." In March 2000 in Lisbon the heads of EU states agreed on a series of steps to achieve a "knowledge-based society." Important criteria are summarized in table 11.1.

Several things are remarkable about these criteria. First, the specification of numerical targets five and ten years into the future and of procedures to achieve them recalls, if not Stalinist five-year plans,

This chapter is based on A. Alesina and R. Perotti, 2004, The European Union: A politically incorrect view, *Journal of Economic Perspective* (Fall), pp. 27–48.

Table 11.1
Criteria for a knowledge-based society

• Employment rate: overall 67% (2005), 70% (2010); women 57% (2005), 60% (2010); older workers 50%
• Long-term unemployment prevention: every young and adult unemployed to be offered a fresh start in 6 or 12 months respectively
• Proportion of unemployed participating in active measures: 20%
• Increase of effective average exit age: by 5 years
• Reduction of school dropout rate: 10% at EU level and half 2000 percentage in each member state
• Raising educational attainments of 25–64 years olds: 80%
• Participation of adults in education and training: 15% at EU level and no member state below 10%
• Coverage of childcare services 0–3: 33%
• Coverage of childcare services 3–6: 90%

Source: Alesina and Perotti (2004).

at least the industrial policies of the 1970s. As table 11.1 shows, in 2010 Europe is supposed to achieve, among other targets, a certain level of labor force participation, a certain rate of long-term unemployment, a certain level of enrollment of children in pre-schools (for different ages of children), a certain level of population involved in adult training programs. Second, all the numerical targets are the same for every country; cultural or preference diversity across countries is irrelevant. Consider, for instance, participation of women in the labor force and childcare. These are issues in which significant cultural differences certainly come into play.

Third, controversial proposals for government intervention are presented as self-evident truths. For instance, academic research has raised serious concerns about the cost effectiveness of adult training programs, but this evidence is ignored because it runs contrary to the European passion for government programs. Fourth, the dirigiste rhetoric is remarkable. We give a typical example of European policy discourse, from the Commission's proposal for a Council recommendation on the Italian employment policies for

2002: "[Italy should take] measures to increase labor market flexibility and modernize work organization, while promoting the synergy between flexibility and security and avoiding marginalization of disadvantaged persons." We doubt that anyone has a clear idea of what is meant by this Eurocratic language but we can conjecture that it is something about Italy's needing more labor market flexibility, but without firing workers. Indeed it is standard for every policy statement in favor of market freedom to be immediately followed by an acknowledgment of the problems of excessive competition, and a call in favor of protection of those who may be temporarily affected by a sweeping reform, and so on.

We submit a second example, an excerpt from the Lisbon decision on cultural policy and research, in table 11.2. Because the European Council controls research funds in Europe, it sets the research priorities. It is one of these priorities in the area of social sciences that we quote in the table. Pomposity of the rhetoric aside, the attitude toward a creative activity like research is astonishing. The directive sets priorities for researchers based on what the Council expects from them. Note the reference to a so-called European social model, which implies that research not sympathetic with this model is not welcome and will not be funded.

The third example has to do with the coordination of fiscal policy. Since the introduction of the euro there has been an ongoing struggle between Brussels, whose aim is to impose the same deficit policy on all member countries, and the states' desires to move in different directions, in particular, in regard to large deficits. The (in)famous Growth and Stability Pact required member countries to keep their deficits below 3 percent of GDP. This pact is often called more appropriately the Stability Pact because of its focus on stable budgets. The word "growth" was added after the then French Prime Minister Lionel Jospin considered it too conservative (Anglo Saxon) to talk about macroeconomic stability alone without a reference to growth. In any case, in addition to the basic 3 percent deficit

Table 11.2
EU criteria for European social scientists

(i) Knowledge-based society and social cohesion
The building of a European knowledge society is a clear political objective for the
European Community. The research aims to provide the basis of understanding
needed to ensure this takes place in a manner which accords with specific
European conditions and aspirations.
• Improving the generation, distribution and use of knowledge and its impact on
economic and social development [. . .]. Research will focus on: characteristics of
knowledge and its functioning in relation to the economy and society, as well as
for innovation and for entrepreneurial activities; and the transformation of
economic and social institutions; the dynamics of knowledge production,
distribution and use, role of knowledge codification and impact of ICTs; the
importance of territorial structures and social networks in these processes.
• Options and choices for the development of a knowledge-based society [. . .].
Research will focus on: features of a knowledge based society in line with
European social models and the need to improve the quality of life; social and
territorial cohesion [. . .]
• The variety of paths towards a knowledge society. [. . .] Research will focus on:
globalization in relation to pressures for convergence; the implications for
regional variation; challenges to European societies from a diversity of cultures
and increased sources of knowledge [. . .]
(ii) Citizenship, democracy and new forms of governance
The work will identify the main factors influencing changes in governance and
citizenship, in particular in the context of increased integration and globalization
and from the perspectives of history and cultural heritage [. . .]. Research will
focus on: relationships between integration, enlargement and institutional change
within the context of their historical evolution and with a comparative
perspective [. . .]
The research activities carried out within this thematic priority area will include
exploratory research at the leading edge of knowledge on subjects closely related
to one or more topics within it. Two complementary approaches will be utilized:
one receptive and open—the other proactive.

Source: Alesina and Perotti (2004). Original source: Council decision of September
30, 2002: Integrating and strengthening the European Research Area (2002–2006),
Official Journal of the European Communities, October 29, 2002, pp. L294/7–L294/8.

requirement, the Council drew up a complex set of rules for monitoring national budgets that included punishing a country if it violates the pact.

In one remarkable case in 2002, there were several week-long negotiations with Ireland on its fiscal policy. The Irish budget is (and was) one of the most solid in Europe. In 2002 Ireland had a surplus and the debt over GDP ratio had fallen from about 120 percent of GDP in 1988 to a comfortable 60 percent of GDP. The Council reprimanded Ireland and started the procedures for imposing monetary penalties. Ireland's fault was to have cut its surplus by about 0.2 percent of GDP: according to the Council, this could have fueled inflation. Ireland was indeed in violation of some rules associated with the deficit management polices set by the European Union. But it is outrageous that there could be a reprimand applied to a country that cut its surplus by 0.2 percent of GDP, especially since a change of 0.2 percent in a budget is pretty close to a rounding error! Even more outrageous was that among the countries reprimanding Ireland was Italy, which at that time had a deficit of about 2 percent of GDP and a debt to GDP ratio of close to 120 percent! The other interesting turn this rather comical event took was that in the phrasing of the reprimand the statements about the effect of taxes and spending on inflation were written with the utmost certainty as if they were laws of nature. These misleading assumptions are indicative of yet another problem with European policy-making. Policy is written as if policy-makers know exactly what causes what, when, and by how much. This, of course, is symptomatic of dirigisme, French style. Also the Stability Pact creates incentives for creative accounting. In some European finance ministries, resources are devoted to the construction of elaborate schemes to shift spending and debt off-budget rather than cut spending. The result is that the stability pact is formally satisfied, but national budgets become increasingly less transparent.

Why are these examples worrisome? One could think of all these activities of target setting, white papers, comments on white papers, reviews, and so on, as a useless but harmless displays of misplaced energy by dirigiste public servants. But it is not quite so simple. Let us begin with the Lisbon process. First, European policy-makers charged with the implementation of the Lisbon Agenda have developed a tendency to see "plans," policy intervention, and public spending as the key ingredients to solve every problem of growth. This target-based approach sets the policy debate in Europe completely on a wrong footing. It makes the European public believe that policy-makers know how to predict (and influence!) such thing as women's participation rates ten years into the future, coverage of preschool for different ages of toddlers, and so on. The impression given is that policy-makers know how to fix things, so it is only a matter of doing more planning and coordinating, devising better procedures, more rules, and more latitude for public intervention, and more white papers. Intellectual logic is what is missing.

To be sure, the Lisbon Agenda, because of its unrealistic targets, has been largely ignored by national politicians in their day-to-day work. The Council at the moment does not have the power to force national governments to adopt the kind of legislation that would directly affect the targets (for example, to open more public preschool facilities). However, the existence of all the planning documents and targets poses the potential danger of enforcement. A particularly aggressive and dirigiste Commission could take the Lisbon Agenda, and the documents that evolved from it, and use them to put pressure on national governments. For instance, the United Kingdom could be made to adopt continental European-style welfare programs, which is why the United Kingdom has been weary of the EU process overall. At the opposite extreme, Scandinavian countries, which also view the EU process suspiciously, could risk losing the welfare state that they know and love, and they certainly do not want anybody interfering with their politics.

The third problem with the Lisbon Agenda is that it is now openly talked about as a failure, which delivers an unnecessary blow to the perception of the entire EU project's ability to set policys goals. By doing so it risks damaging what is good about the European Union, and not only the Lisbon targets set for 2010. Europeans do not need any more gloom and setbacks. The perceived failure of the Lisbon Agenda could in fact be used to increase centralization and create more dirigisme. Adding more government programs when a single one fails is a typical European response.

The case of fiscal policy illustrates the obsession of European politicians in Brussels with coordination of not only monetary and fiscal policy but also the welfare and retirement policies of member countries. "Coordination" is a word loaded with positive connotation in Europe. The best way of running a federation of countries, the argument goes, is to make policies as coordinated as possible. The same Lisbon Agenda targets uniform fiscal policy, all monitored by the European Union. The idea of centralization of policies is by and large a French idea, since France was and largely still is a very centralized country with most decisions made in Paris, whereas Germany has a very different tradition, derived from the relative independence of its regional governments. French top public servants, educated in the Grandes Ecoles, hold many top civil servant jobs in Brussels, and they firmly believe that a good central government can set targets and devise plans. Unfortunately, this mentality is starting to permeate the EU bureaucracy.

As we pointed out in the previous chapter, the issue of coordination should be viewed as a trade-off between the benefits of scale and the heterogeneity of preferences. With a small group of countries it is relatively easier to agree on more policies, even if among the fifteen disagreement is commonplace, as we noted above. With the club extended, much less can be coordinated, since heterogeneity of preferences edges in. At the time of EU enlargement in the early 2000s several observers made the point that European integration faced a trade-off between the processes of deepening and widening. Enlargement, they argued, calls for less centralization, less deepening, but more widening. The message was largely ignored at the top. On the contrary, the EU Commission, headed by Romano Prodi, basked in the glory of enlargement and deepening, envisaging a larger and ever more cohesive Europe, soon to have its own constitution and looking more and more like a federation. That did not last long. The collapse of the proposed constitution came also as a result of the original EU citizens' fear of integrating with the new member states.

In our view, the difficulty of imposing uniform policies on fifteen relatively homogeneous countries, then extending such policies to twenty-five much less homogeneous countries has been vastly underestimated. In fact a positive effect of recent European enlargement is that any move toward heavy dirigisme and excessive centralization will be more difficult.

So we end this chapter where we started. The European Union has had a very positive role in liberalizing markets. Unfortunately, in some policy areas, the EU institutions are being captured by a type of European mentality that sees government policy as a cure-all in many areas. The need for coordination of policies is vastly overemphasized, perhaps strategically, by EU officials, since they will be the ones involved and empowered by the supranational coordination itself.

12 The Euro

Many commentators, policy-makers, and even some economists have implicated the euro and the policies of the European Central Bank (ECB) as behind the low growth, high unemployment and a general economic malaise throughout much of Europe. Italy's former economic minister Giulio Tremonti, for instance, repeatedly blamed the euro for just about every problem in Italy's economy. The ECB is often accused of being so focused on inflation as to stave off any prospect of European recovery.

These perceptions are almost entirely wrong. This chapter explains why and shows how the debate over the euro is nothing more than a red herring that detracts from discussion about the real problems in Europe. To be sure, the euro has created many challenges for European economies, but it is the failure to make adequate structural adjustments that has led to problems, not the euro itself. Blaming the euro is like blaming an exam when you choose to take it, do not prepare for it, and then fail.

Adopting the euro was a major step forward for Europe and a radical move for European politicians who are normally slow when it comes to reforms. On balance, as a cornerstone of European integration, the euro was a good idea. Now that Europe has one currency, the exit of one of the larger countries would be a major blow to the entire concept of European Union. It could also cause substantial financial shocks, depending on how it happens, and exacerbate other structural problems that have slowed growth in Europe. So, understanding how to live with the euro is critical to Europe's well-being.

From a purely economic standpoint, the benefits of a single currency are many: facilitation of trade in goods and services without exchange rate risks and conversion costs; transparency in prices across countries; integration of financial markets; better competition without risk of competitive devaluations whereby one country devalues its currency to make its exports cheaper, generating a chain reaction from competitors leading to inflation; and of course, a European Central Bank committed to price stability, eliminating the risk of high inflation for countries especially prone to falling into inflation spirals. For some countries, like Italy, Spain, Portugal, and Greece, being admitted in the euro area was a symbol of acceptance in a club of countries with respectable macroeconomic policies. The benefits were immediate. Italy's interest payments on its large public debt (about 120 percent of GDP at the moment of entry in the eurozone) immediately fell as interest rates leveled off at the rate of Germany. Elimination of the devaluation risk inherent in the defunct Lira was the single most important factor for the improvement of Italian public finances. Failure to enter the euro area would have pushed the high interest rates and high deficits even higher and likely catapulted Italy to a default on its public debt. This would have had significant negative implications not only for Italian financial stability but also for Europe overall.

The costs were clear as well. Adopting the euro has meant the loss of national independence in domestic monetary policy and of exchange rate flexibility. In the euro area monetary and interest rate polices are chosen by the European Central Bank, which has to pay attention to the average macroeconomic variables of the entire euro area. If a country grows less than the average, it cannot demand a more expansionary monetary policy, and if a country's inflation is above average it cannot obtain a more restrictive monetary policy. For this reason economists who subscribe to the belief that monetary policy is an important tool in the fine-tuning of the economy are apt to point to the euro as a problem.

Disagreement among economists over the euro has essentially boiled down to different weights attached to the pros and cons noted above. The pessimists predicted that at the first sign of a euro area recession, the asymmetries among member countries and the politically palatable idea of competitive devaluations would increase tensions among members and strain the euro area agreements. In some ways this has happened. A few prominent politicians now blame the euro for the sluggish growth of their country. As a result some minor and more careless politicians have openly suggested abandoning the euro. Some economists like Harvard's Martin Feldstein and Nobel Prize winner Milton Friedman had predicted that the adoption of the euro would greatly intensify political conflicts among European countries and even increase the probability of wars. The darkest predictions about inter-European conflicts were exaggerations, but European politicians sometimes do lament the straitjacket of a common monetary policy.

The optimists, in contrast, point to the prime example of the United States where there are differences in regional growth and no pressure to return to regional currencies. Of course, the political unity of the United States is much stronger. It is worth noting that the United States was not born with a single currency. It took several decades of political unity before a common currency was introduced, as the pessimists have pointed out. In many ways the economists were right in identifying the pros and cons of the euro; the facts have confirmed the middle-of-the-road view. The most naïvely optimistic analysis, which predicted that the euro would be a sort of great leap forward for Europe, turned out to be wrong, and so has the most pessimistic one, which predicted immediate failure of the euro with significant tension among members.

In the realm of politics, again there were two camps. Those who pushed for the euro on political grounds were the (naïve) European enthusiasts for whom more coordination and more unity are always better, by definition. They argued that a single currency would push member countries to adopt more uniform policies, a clear blessing by definition. As we showed in the previous chapter, coordination is good in some areas, but it is not "good by definition" in all areas of economic policy. Still, the introduction of the single currency was used to justify calls for coordination of a variety of policies, many of which have nothing to do with the single currency. Others made the more pertinent argument that the euro would increase the incentives to adopt those structural reforms necessary to promote growth, since competitive devaluations and monetary fixes would no longer be available. They further contended that the euro would greatly enhance competition within Europe, adding pressure for structural reforms. The pessimists argued that the only result of the euro would be to shut down a channel of policy flexibility without generating any positive response in the structural, supply side, and competition areas.

Once again (leaving aside the naïve euro enthusiasts) the debate was right in identifying conflicting forces. In the end, the middle of the road, more moderate view turned out to be correct. The adoption of the euro did create an impetus for more European integration, an impetus that could and should have been better used in one area alone: the creation of a true single market for goods and services, including financial intermediaries. European governments were slow in these areas, and some even pushed back. Meanwhile the European Commission used the euro as an excuse to push for more integration in a variety of areas where integration is not necessary, or even harmful, as we discussed in chapters 10 and 11.

The commission, for instance, erred in envisioning a monetary union of closely coordinated fiscal policies. The need for fiscal coordination was exaggerated in Brussels and on some occasions has even proved to be counterproductive, as we discussed in the previous chapter with the example regarding Ireland. In fact one may even argue the opposite, namely that given the fact that monetary policy is the same for every country in the eurozone, what is needed, rather than coordination, is *more* rather than less fiscal flexibility.

And what about the prediction of the euro optimists that having shut down domestic monetary polices, European countries would push forward into the area of structural reforms, namely labor, goods, and services markets reforms? By reducing various rigidities, these reforms would have allowed economies to respond more quickly to negative shocks. This, however, did not happen with enough swiftness and depth. As we discussed in chapter 4, a few countries did introduce some labor market reforms (Denmark, Sweden, and to a much lesser extent Italy and Germany). Others like France did very little, but overall the pace of structural reforms in Europe has been too slow and too timid. In the area of services, from finance to gas and electricity reform has been particularly disappointing.

The sluggish pace of supply-side reforms is the reason for the current economic difficulties of Europe, not the euro. It is true that the euro makes life in nonreforming countries more difficult: devaluations that for a while stimulate exports even in less competitive economies are no longer available. But this is a benefit because it should create more incentives for reforms and eliminate the temptation of competitive devaluations that are like an addictive drug for the economy.

Thus, seven years after the introduction of the euro we are starting to see some worrisome signs. First, rather than an impulse to

speed up reforms, the euro is accompanied by renewed protectionism. In France, in particular, suspending the rules of the internal
market, which prohibit state aid to firms, is viewed by all politicians, independently of their ideology, as an acceptable, rather
desirable way to protect French industry and to "pick technology
champions," by subsidizing them. In Portugal the economic situation is getting increasingly difficult, and the solutions are not immediately obvious. Fueled by a consumption boom following entry
into the euro area, and the fall in interest rates, Portuguese nominal
wages have risen in seven years a total of 30 percent. Inflation has
eroded two-thirds of this gain, but still real wages have grown
almost 10 percent. Since productivity has been flat, this increase in
real wages has translated into an increase in unit labor costs (29
percent). Italy has done only slightly better: nominal wages are up
21 percent, unit labor costs up 18 percent, and real wages up 3.2
percent. No surprise if Portugal and Italy have a hard time exporting! In these countries, especially in Italy, China has become the evil
cause of all economic problems, but the reality is that Italy and Portugal are losing ground against Germany, where in seven years unit
labor costs have increased by 3.4 percent only, and Germany is
happily increasing its exports to China. Chinese roads are full of
Audis, driven, amongst others, by the numerous Chinese bureaucrats who have the right to an official car.

These developments raise two questions. How did Portugal and
Italy (and Spain is on its way to a similar situation) get into this
mess, how can they get out, and is there a risk that the way out
might be an exit from the euro? Starting from the reasons why they
got in this mess, one underlying factor is the lack of competition in
the service sector, which has fueled inflation throughout the
economy. Consider again Italy. Since it joined the euro, the price of
banking services has increased 38 percent (more than 5 percent per
year), auto insurance 31 percent, and hotels and restaurants 18

and 15 percent respectively, while industrial prices have increased less than 6 percent, or 1.5 percent per year. The increase in the price of uncompetitive local services squeezes the purchasing power of wages. Workers try to make up by demanding wage increases, but the euro and global competition do not allow firms to pass wage increases onto prices. Profits are squeezed (except those of banks and insurance companies, of course) and firms are in trouble.

Another factor has been the virtual freeze of productivity growth, in part due to lack of innovation, a topic we discussed in chapter 5, and in part the result of the slowdown produced by rising costs. Moreover these countries have maintained an industrial structure that is particularly vulnerable to competition from the new exports coming from Southeast Asia.

In the past a round of devaluation would have put Portugal and Italy out of economic crisis—at least for some time. Under the euro, the only way out is real wage moderation and a sharp increase in productivity. Neither is easy. In Portugal the government has just announced a grandiose plan of public investment in infrastructure and R&D, dreaming that new infrastructure will be enough to attract foreign direct investment and jump-start productivity growth. In Italy tariffs and import quotas have become the common language of politicians. The most likely outcome, as we observed, is slow growth. But with such a prospect, will Italy's commitment to the euro survive? Why suffer through a recession if a devaluation can cut real wages overnight? Portugal needs to give up the 10 percent increase in real wages that was not justified by higher productivity—and perhaps even more.

Along with the euro, the ECB is becoming another target in Europe's inability to address its real problems. Rather than attacking the entrenched political power of various insiders—labor unions, monopolistic firms, inside traders in financial markets—

that prevent the adoption of reforms, European politicians often attack the ECB.

The ECB has been accused first of not defending the euro enough when in the Fall of 2000 the euro fell to about 0.85 euro against the U.S. dollar. At that time some euro enthusiasts jumped on the opportunity to make the (peculiar) argument that the weakness of the euro was due to lack of political unity of Europe. Then, not so long ago, the ECB was accused of not preventing the euro from appreciating too much when it reached about 1.3 against the dollar. (Was there perhaps "too much" political unity now?) More generally, the ECB has been accused of being too obsessed with inflation and not concerned enough about growth. These accusations continue to be made even when real interest rates in the eurozone were about zero and below.

The allegation of the ECB's failure is unfair. No one and no institution is perfect, and the ECB could do well to invest in more communication skills with the public. But its monetary policy in Europe has been reasonable, so it cannot be made in any way responsible for the lackluster economic performance of the region. However, while the policies at the ECB have been middle of the road, its rhetoric has been mishandled. At every occasion the ECB keeps repeating that its only goal is price stability, without explaining that this is the same as keeping demand at a level close to the level of the economy's potential output growth. The ECB should make some rhetorical allowance for its role (which undoubtedly is present) in keeping an eye on European growth.

Attacks on the ECB have come from two sides: government officials interested in deflecting criticism directed at their inability to handle the real problems of Europe, and some economists intent on concentrating on the demand side of the economy while ignoring that the underlying cause of Europe's problems is on the supply side. The first group of critics tries to convince their electorate that one of the main reasons for Europe's sluggish growth and high unemployment is the tight monetary policy of the ECB, which is too obsessed with inflation. The second group of critics often compares the ECB with the Fed in negative terms: the Fed is viewed as the champion of US growth, the ECB the culprit for European stagnation. This comparison overemphasizes the role of monetary policy in promoting and maintaining sustained growth and exaggerates the achievements of the Fed when compared with the alleged failures of the ECB. In fact one could argue that the Fed was too loose and has contributed to creating a bubble in some markets (like the housing market) because of very low interest rates for many years. Monetary policy is a powerful tool for macroeconomic management in the short run, but remember these words: short run. The impending decline of Europe is not a short-run problem; there is nothing monetary policy can do to prevent it.

So was the euro a good or a bad idea? In our view, on balance the adoption of the euro has been a good idea. An area as economically integrated like Europe can greatly benefit from the elimination of exchange rate risk, conversion costs, more relative price transparency, and easier financial communications. Absent the euro and the reduction in interest rates that it has brought about, some countries (such as Italy and Greece) might have fallen into a financial crisis and dragged their neighbors into a financial mess. The current problems of European economies do not stem from the euro but from the lack of those accompanying supply-side and competition measures that would have permitted the euro to display fully its beneficial effects.

It is too premature to assume that the euro will last forever, and that under no condition should Europeans consider giving it up. If reforms are postponed much longer, and stagnation continues, the anti-euro rhetoric that we occasionally see today will spread. The exit of some countries from the currency union is not inconceivable although unlikely. This would be a major blow not only to the countries that exit but to the very project of a single European currency.

13   Budget Fixes

Often countries that do not grow enough and are in need of reform find themselves in a bind because of their public finances. On the one hand, they have deficits; on the other hand, some of the necessary remedies, such as tax reductions, can make the deficits worse. Sometimes pension reforms that bring large budget savings in the long run create deficits in the short run. Often even if necessary reforms do not cost public money (labor market liberalization, the elimination of trade barriers in some sectors, etc.), some compensation scheme must be set in place to reduce or alleviate the cost that the reforms impose on some individuals. But the wrong budget fixes, like marginal tax hikes, can deter growth. This is why fixing the budget, something that many countries in Europe need to do, can deeply entangle implementation of growth-enhancing reforms.

In the past many countries, on both sides of the Atlantic, found it difficult to keep their budgets in order, and periodically large budget deficits appeared. In the late 1970s and 1980s large budget deficits were the rule rather than the exception. Then came a period of deficit reductions (see figure 13.1); today the deficits have returned.

In 2004 the United States had a budget deficit of 4 percent of GDP, whereas at the end of the 1990s it had a surplus of 1.3 percent of GDP. Countries of the euro area had an average deficit of 2.8 percent

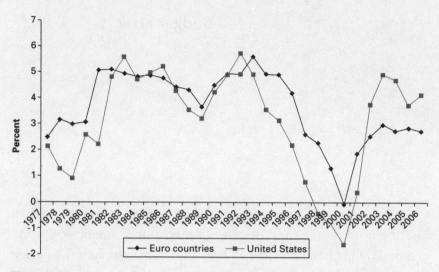

Figure 13.1
Deficit to GDP ratios of the European Union and the United States since 1975. 2005 and 2006 are projections. Source: *OECD Economic Outlook*, December 1995.

of GDP, with the biggest offenders being Italy with 3.2 percent and next France and Germany with 3.7 percent. Some of these deficits are growing bigger.

Before proceeding further, we must dispel the wrong impression that budget deficits are always a problem, and that they must be avoided at all costs. This is not the case. Temporary budget deficits are part of the tool kit of a good policy-maker. During recessions, budget deficits are likely to appear because tax revenues are temporarily low. It would be a mistake to raise tax rates in a recession to balance the budget. Also, if government spending is temporarily high, say, because of a war or a natural calamity, it is a mistake to have a short-term spike in tax rates to keep a balanced budget every year. Budget deficits (and surpluses) have a useful role in smoothing temporary fluctuations in tax revenues and spending. Obviously deficits become a problem when they are long lasting; they create large debts and are a sign of a permanent inability to keep spending in line with taxation.

While the levels of deficit in the United States and Europe are currently similar, the reasons for them are very different. The current US deficit is due to three factors having relatively equal weight: the wars in Afghanistan and Iraq, the tax cuts implemented by President George W. Bush in his first term, and increases in nonmilitary spending, especially in health care. The two wars aside, to most economists both the tax cuts and the increase in nonmilitary spending have seemed excessive, especially in light of a looming social security deficit. In the case of Europe the current deficits are the result of governments' inability to control current spending and the effect a prolonged period of low growth on tax revenues.

Fiscal tightening was associated with the creation of the monetary union, but soon after the adoption of the euro the major continental economies slipped back to running large deficits. Admission to the euro area required a deficit level below 3 percent of GDP, and a debt level below 60 percent of GDP; the debt level, however, was largely ignored. Most countries were above 60 percent, and Italy and Belgium were admitted with a debt level twice that size! The deficit criterion was enforced, and some argue that it was motivated explicitly as a way to keep fiscally fragile Italy out of the union. Nevertheless Italy eventually was admitted. Shortly after the creation of the monetary union, the Stability and Growth Pact prescribed rules for fiscal balance. But the Pact, too, after a few years was violated by member countries Italy, France, Germany, and Portugal. Despite various attempts at enforcing fiscal rules, in practice, no rules are observed today, even though the European Commission and Ecofin in Brussels act as if they are, and have meetings with economic ministers and bureaucrats of member countries and reprimand them routinely for their deficits. Although EU countries negotiate with Brussels on what is or is not acceptable as a deficit, the results are mixed on compliance. Our impression is that at this time the large countries in Europe can do just about anything they please with deficits.

In addition to current deficits, both the United States and the European countries face long-term fiscal problems: in the area of health care especially in the United States, and in the area of pensions in continental Europe. The largest "holes" in the pension system are in Germany. Debates about how to reform German pensions have lasted a decade, but so far nothing has been done. While politicians drag their feet, concerned that decisive pension reform might lose them votes, the German people are worried. Research by one of us (Giavazzi) into the behavior of German households shows that those who are most worried about the sustainability of the current welfare system save more, work more, and consume less. In Germany a person aged 35 who is relatively more concerned about the inability of the government to address the sustainability of the pension system has a 6 percent higher savings rate than someone who is less concerned. At age 55 the savings rate increases by almost a quarter. Europeans are not naïve: they understand what may lie ahead.

Americans have used tax cuts to stimulate the economy and perhaps, as some argue, even too much. It is very difficult for European countries to apply the fiscal stimulus of tax cuts. Most European countries have large government sectors (the European average of government spending is close to 50 percent of GDP). Some have large accumulated debt that can become fiscally burdensome if interest rates move up from the current very low rates. In the United States, periods of tax cuts in the early 1960s, mid-1980s, and early 2000s were followed by accelerated growth, so tax cuts greatly helped close up the deficits. The deficits accumulated in the 1980s turned into a surplus by the end of the 1990s almost exclusively due to the sustained and prolonged period of expansion. President Clinton kept spending under control, but he did not have to implement draconian measures or increase tax rates much in order to achieve a surplus. This was precisely because in the 1990s the US economy was growing at exceptionally sustained rates. Be aware, this argument does not imply a simple-minded supply-side economics—namely that tax cuts pay for themselves, so lowering tax rates increases revenues. Rather, it is well-designed tax cuts that stimulate growth, and the spending cuts needed to keep a budget balanced do not have to be exceedingly large.

France, Germany, and Italy face much tougher problems than the United States. Their inability to significantly reduce spending, coupled with low growth, required heavy taxation that has created disincentives for people to work and invest. As we mentioned in chapter 3, high marginal tax rates in Europe are at least in part responsible for the prolonged decline in hours worked and in participation rates in the labor force in continental Europe.

Can Europe afford significant tax cuts? Yes, but only if they are accompanied by offsetting government spending cuts. Will these spending cuts have adverse economic consequences? And are they politically feasible?

On the first question, the evidence on fiscal adjustments in the late 1980s up to the mid-1990s in many OECD countries has provided researchers with a wealth of data on the effects of large changes in fiscal policy. These data show, in particular, what works and what does not work as a fiscal fix. The following are some interesting lessons.

First, deficit reductions in OECD countries that are based on spending cuts have a much better chance of lasting than those based on tax increases. In general, spending cuts lead to more permanent adjustments of the budget than tax increases. Why? Blocking the automatic growth of many spending programs, especially entitlements, is a necessary condition in consolidation a budget, whereas tax increases only temporarily fill a gap. Spending cuts also signal that a government has a serious attitude toward correcting fiscal spending and expectations for lowering interest rates. Lower interest rates help fix a budget.

Second, among the spending cuts, those areas where there is better chance of achieving lasting budget consolidation are public employment (reduction in the growth of wages and/or reduction in the number of public employees) and transfer programs. These are the categories of public spending more prone to increase automatically, so stopping their growth is particularly beneficial and a condition sine qua non for long-lasting consolidations. The problem is that in Europe extraordinary job security for public employees makes it very difficult to cut their numbers and aggressive and powerful unions are very good at obtaining salary increases. The evolution of entitlement programs is, of course, a problem on both sides of the Atlantic: this is why public pension reforms and health care reforms are big issues today.

Third, fiscal adjustments based on spending cuts are less likely (than those based on tax increases) to create recessions, even in the short run. This is a result sometimes referred to as the "non-Keynesian effects" of fiscal policy. It suggests that it is possible to eliminate budget deficits without creating a downturn in growth and, in fact, the sustained growth during the adjustment process helps the adjustment itself by sustaining tax revenue. How is this possible? On the demand side, permanent reductions in government spending signal a decline in future revenue needs for the government, so the consumer feels richer and therefore keeps on consuming. Because expected taxes go down, the expected (before-tax) take-home income goes up. Further, the signal of fiscal toughness by the government may reduce interest rates, stimulating investment. On the supply side, there are additional significant effects. Lower taxes reduce the disincentive to work and lower cost of labor for firms. Conversely, higher taxes discourage labor participation, and higher taxes on income often translate into a demand for higher before-tax wages, to compensate for lower after-tax wages, thus creating higher labor costs for firms. In unionized economies cuts (or slow growth) of public wages and public employment can further translate into wage moderation in the private sector as well, leading to a reduction in labor costs, increased profitability, and more investment spending. The reason is that in unionized labor markets wage increases in the public sector can influence the bargaining power behind unions' demands in the private sector. Indeed, several episodes of large fiscal consolidations have been followed not only by sustained private consumption but also by an investment boom, and as a consequence the economy experienced sustained growth even during the fiscal fix.

The quintessential example of a successful, long-lasting, and expansionary fiscal adjustment is that of Ireland is 1987–89. In about five years Ireland went from a deficit of almost 6 percent of GDP to a surplus of more than 2 percent. Primary expenditures (excluding interest payments) were cut by about 8 percent of GDP, from 43 to 35 percent. Revenues were kept basically constant, and they even slightly declined as a share of GDP. Public employment was cut by 10 percent (from 300,000 to 270,000 public employees). In the same years GDP growth in Ireland jumped from 0 to almost 6 percent a year. Unemployment fell from 10 to 8 percent. Since then, Ireland has become the tiger of Europe, growing much more than any other EU country. This success was facilitated by a devolution of the currency.

An earlier example of a successful and expansionary fiscal adjustment based on spending cuts is Denmark. In 1982 to 1983 Denmark went through an experience similar to that of Ireland. A similar example is Australia in 1986 to 1987. Common to all these cases is that the reforms were carried out swiftly. Decisive action is necessary to change people's confidence in government and the economy. If people do not perceive that fiscal consolidation will be accompanied by an improvement in the economy, consumer and business confidence will decline. Both are necessary to avoid a slowdown.

Italy took the opposite direction. Starting in the early 1990s, Italy initiated a long series of deficit cuts as a way of satisfying the fiscal

criteria for joining the European monetary union. The fiscal adjustment was gradual and occurred almost exclusively on the revenue
side. Fiscal revenues as a share of GDP grew from 39 percent in 1987
to 47 percent in 1999 when Italy was admitted into the European
Union. Since then revenues have remained above 45 percent of GDP.
Throughout this period growth was sluggish in Italy, and in 2005,
with a deficit projected to be around 4 percent of GDP and a public
debt increasing toward 120 percent of GDP, Italian public finances
are again in trouble and almost as bad as when the adjustment
started. The Italian fiscal adjustments of the 1990s were not focused
on structural cuts in public spending, so current spending (excluding interest payments) has recently increased to almost two percentage points of GDP. This result is illustrative of precisely the
point we made earlier: the fiscal adjustment did not last because the
government was unable to reduce spending structurally.

Let us now turn to the question of political feasibility. If certain
types of fiscal adjustments (those based on structural spending cuts)
can be successful and long lasting, why does government after government struggle over this very issue?

To begin with, paradoxically, the introduction of the euro has
reduced the pressure on governments to keep their fiscal houses in
order. Italy, once again, is a case in point. Before joining the monetary union, Italy faced high interest rates, rising with the deterio-
rating fiscal policy. The Lira came under pressure every time
financial markets started fluctuating because of the Italian debt.
However, within the monetary union the interest rate of a highly
indebted country, like Italy, is only marginally higher than that of
fiscally virtuous countries, like Finland or Ireland. Italy feels less
pressure because borrowing is cheap. It is even surprising how little
interest rates vary on government debts of the different country
members of the European Union. There are two explanations. One
is that the ECB, when it buys and sells government bonds (the so-

called open-market operations), does not make a distinction between bonds issued by different EU countries: this procedure is probably dictated more by politics than by economics. The second is that private investors may not be worried yet about excessive deficits and debts in Europe. But the problem is that they may stay calm for a while and then suddenly panic and unload bonds, which would have immediate effects on the issuing country's interest rates. Thus so far politicians have found relatively little pressure from the markets toward fiscal rectitude, a dangerous situation indeed.

Still, although politicians may not perceive the economic costs of deficits, they are all very much aware of the potential political costs of fiscal adjustments. It is widely believed that a government that implements a tight fiscal policy will lose the following election. But this belief is nothing more than one of those stylized facts, so called because they do not survive close statistical scrutiny. Among the several studies on the consequences of fiscal policy, none has found convincing evidence that reducing budget deficits has significant electoral costs. The more relevant political constraint is related to the issue of concentrated costs and diffuse benefits. Taxpayers overall benefit from spending cuts when taxes are reduced or not increased. However, when preparing budgets, European governments must bargain more or less formally with various types of organizations—unions, business groups, farmers, and so on. The main interest of each organization is to defend its favorite spending programs and the "favors" they receive from the government—pensions for labor unions, wages for public sector unions, subsidies for farmers and business associations, and so on. Taxpayers are never represented at these bargaining tables. Therefore organizations that have an interest in opposing spending cuts get more political representation than taxpayers. The result is obvious: spending cuts are difficult to implement.

The discussions between government and certain socioeconomic groups can be productive, as is more typical of Scandinavian countries, where they are consensus oriented and coordinated within a macroeconomic policy framework. Another less beneficial approach is the "free-for-all" fight of myriad groups interested in defending and expanding their share of the spending. In both systems there is a tendency to favor tax increases over spending cuts, but the second system is of course much more deleterious.

There is also an ideological component to European public opinion on discussions of public spending. Whether the right or the left, European politicians and voters are convinced of two things: (1) even relatively minor cuts in government spending will push Europe into a savage US style capitalism; (2) any cut in government spending is recessionary.

The first tenet is deeply embedded in the European view of the role of government, as we discussed in chapter 1. Several decades of ever-expanding welfare programs have convinced Europeans that the government is essential for their well-being. They tend to underestimate how markets can provide some services more efficiently than government, from education to forms of insurance. But political strategy is involved as well. Powerful public sector unions have an incentive to make everyone believe that even the smallest cut in the number of public employees will throw the country in disarray. For instance, teacher unions like the public to think that their number cannot be reduced, despite the lower birth rate in Europe; otherwise, the educational system will collapse, so they claim.

On the second point, the prevalence of a strict and excessively dogmatic Keynesianism (that is, the advocacy of monetary and fiscal programs by government to increase employment and spending) has led to an overestimation of the effects of demand-side policies and an underestimation of the supply-side effects of tax distortions. Many European economists are deeply entrenched in this view, believing that more aggregate demand and, in particular, a more expansionary monetary and fiscal policy is all that Europe needs.

Entangled in this view is that the solution to every problem is more government spending. Take public investments in infrastructure. They are the cure-alls of European politicians and commentators, as if lack of infrastructure is a problem in Europe. In most European countries airports, roads, and public transportation are at least just as good as, or even better than, in the United States. In the case of education at the universities, as we discussed in chapter 5, what is needed in Europe is not more money but better incentives, more competition, and more private money. But all that is heard in Europe is the call for more public money for strictly public universities.

In summary, if Europeans want to get serious about fiscal consolidation, they should cut spending as a share of GDP by a few percentage points. They should make cuts in public employment and wages and in entitlement programs. These cuts can reduce the marginal tax rates and thus have positive effects on the supply side.

Table 13.1
Percentage of individuals at risk of poverty, 2003

Country	Before social transfers	After social transfers
Sweden	29	11
Finland	29	11
Netherlands	22	12
Denmark	32	12
Germany	24	16
France	26	12
Belgium	29	16
Austria	24	13
Italy	22	19
Spain	22	19
Greece	24	21
Ireland	31	21
United Kingdom	26	18

Source: Eurostat.

As is often observed by many economists, but forgotten in policy debates, large government does not necessarily mean efficient government. The Swedish welfare state is able to reduce the percentage of households at risk of poverty from 29 (before social transfer) to 9. In Italy where the size of government is only a few percentage points of GDP smaller than Sweden, social transfers to households at risk of poverty are almost negligible: from 22 to 19 percent (Eurostat data). So large government does not always mean good government, and countries can reduce government spending without increasing inequality. This message is critical for Europe to remember.

14   A Wake-up Call for
                      Europeans

Are Europeans blissfully unaware of the problems and challenges
that we have sketched in this book? Certainly not. Concerns for
the sustainability of the welfare state, for the effects of competition
from Asia, for the demographic and migration pressures coming
from eastern Europe and northern Africa, for the brain drain that
causes Europe to lose many of its best students and researchers to
the United States are widespread. The fact that over time little has
been done to address these problems is frightening, and some
people are induced to save more and consume less, compounding
the problems of the European economy.

Politicians, however, rather than work together to solve these
problems, reassure voters by promising "protection"—protection
from Chinese imports, protection from the cultural diversity that
comes with immigration, protection from the superior technology
of some American firms, protection of university jobs, protection of
rich farmers, of small shopkeepers, of wealthy notary publics, of the
unemployed, of the poor, of the old.

The word "protection" can have a positive connotation: protection of the weaker, protection from aggression, protection from
adversity. But the kind of protection to which we are referring is of
a different nature. It is the protection of insiders, of those who are
connected, at the expense of those who would benefit from more
competition. It is protection of the few against the interests of the

many. Often the two kinds of protection are strategically mixed up, and insiders use this confusion to protect privilege. For example, think of labor protection laws. As we discussed in chapter 4, labor protection is "sold" to the public as a way of protecting the weaker, that is, the workers against the business interests of management. In practice they are instead a way of protecting older, unionized workers and denying entry of newcomers into the labor market.

The epicenter of protectionism is in France. In his recent book *The World as I See It*, Lionel Jospin, the former prime minister, attacks what he calls a "new caste" of financiers, industrialists, top civil servants, and privileged journalists for promoting globalization at the expense of ordinary workers. Meanwhile in France the unemployment rate has increased from 8.4 percent at the beginning of the 2000 decade to 9.5 percent last year (2005). Over the same period in Britain unemployment fell from 5.5 to 4.7 percent. Protectionism reminds us of the Great Depression, which started with the stock market crash of 1929 and led to a burst of protectionism that aggravated the crisis itself and contributed to creating the economic and political conditions that degenerated into the Second World War. Jospin is on the left, but when it comes to reassure citizens that all is well, nothing needs change, the problems all lie with globalization and the inhuman "Anglo-Saxon" social model, while France can do better, and differences between the left and the right become obfuscated. Presidential candidate Nicolas Sarkozy, the most prominent French politician on the right, likes to make rhetorical statements about the need for reforms. But when the privileges of French farmers are in danger, he lashes out at any attempt by Brussels to agree on tariff reductions with the United States. If he is unable to resist the pressure of farmers, which represent a tiny fraction of all voters, how can we trust his ability to take on any other interest group, which is the necessary step for serious reforms?

But protectionism is in vogue elsewhere, not only in France. The former economic minister of Italy, Giulio Tremonti, has published a book, *Rischi fatali*, in which he argues that all of Italy's problems can be ascribed to the euro and to China's entry into the WTO, and that Italy needs to be protected from both. Günter Verheugen, the German commissioner for industry in Brussels, never stops advocating that for the "European champions" antitrust rules should be "applied with caution." Italy leads the world in the protection of domestic inefficient banks; the Protuguese response to the mess the country is in is to focus on a project of rather useless infrastructure investment. Economic protectionism is only the tip of the iceberg. Spain's former prime minister, José Maria Aznar, thinks that Europeans should rediscover their "Christian roots and cultural values, and set aside the enormous error of multiculturalism, a failed experiment," which he links to the rise of terrorism. No wonder people worry and look after their savings.

It is nevertheless unfair to treat Europeans as unanimous in their thinking about protectionism. In the United Kingdom, Tony Blair and Gordon Brown, although political opposites, have been staunch supporters of openness. Even within continental Europe not all voices are uniformly protectionist. There is, especially around the European Commission, recognition that the problem is too much, not too little, protection. The Commission has fought hard, and successfully, for competition policy, as we discussed in chapter 6. The most pronounced exposition of this view is the Sapir Report (July 2003), a document of the European Commission written by a group of European economists that has received wide attention in Europe.

The report correctly identifies most of the problems that Europe faces, but in its proposals it suffers from the typical European syndrome. First, it confuses major and minor problems in a lengthy list of measures that it proposes. Some are indeed important, and some are of minor relevance. So it offers politicians the option of choosing what is least politically costly and postponing the really important decisions. The report, for instance, goes through the fine print of the Growth and Stability Pact, explaining in detail the changes to European fiscal rules. As we discussed in chapter 6, this is unlikely to make a difference. Second, the report suggests that the solution to many problems lies in more government spending, research and infrastructure, for example. This is not right. In the case of research and universities, a big spending item in the Sapir Report, we have already shown in chapter 5 that throwing more money at European universities without changing the rules will simply fatten the rents that many European academics enjoy. The solution is not to spend more public money but to charge families for the cost of education and allow private universities to compete with the public ones. As for primary and secondary education, it is far from obvious that Europe spends too little public money on education. The average European public high school probably offers a better education than the comparable American high school. Further, within Europe, the countries that spend more on education do not necessarily produce better education. But money is not the entire problem. Teachers are typically protected by very strong public sector unions that impose job security, which of course lowers the incentive to do a better job.

Obsession with infrastructure is the other big spending item in the Sapir Report. What does the call for infrastructure growth refer to? Europe's economic disease cannot be due to lack of fast trains. Compare the Acela, a so-called fast train, which takes almost four hours to cover the less than 400 kms between Boston and New York, with the French TGV. Is New York's Kennedy airport more functional than Frankfurt's airport? Hardly. Is Interstate 95 that runs down the US East Coast connecting Boston, New York, Philadelphia, Washington, and then down to Florida better kept than the German highways? No way.

So, what does Europe urgently need? We close the book with a short list of what we believe are the priorities. We have six proposals that are sufficiently sharp to allow politicians little room for selecting the least costly. The order in which we present them should not be taken as an indication of what needs to be done first.

1. *Liberalization of product and service markets*   For financial services, namely banks, responsibility for supervision should be transferred to a European authority, modeled along the lines of the British Financial Services Authority. The new institution should be independent of the Commission (to avoid the risk of political pressure) and also independent of the ECB, so as not to involve the ECB in the problems arising from possible bank defaults. To address the conflicts of interest discussed in chapter 9, this new institution should consider whether to impose a separation between banks and mutual funds, as Israel has recently done. But liberalization cannot and should not come only from Brussels. Zoning rules, clearly a national prerogative, should be reconsidered in order to open up the market for distribution to large international firms, like the model of Walgreen, Target, and the CVS drugstores. Restrictions on the distribution of selected products, by licensed pharmacies, for example, should be lifted. Access to professions should be liberalized by removing the laws by which many European states regulate professional services. The companies that provide gas, telephone services, and electricity should be kept from owning the networks through which these services travel. When networks are owned by the incumbents, entry is difficult and the incumbents never face serious competition. Since the critical nodes in a network are those that connect one country with another, networks' regulation should, as in the case of financial services and for similar reasons, be transferred to a European body. Also no real competition can emerge if the largest utilities are owned or controlled by the state or local governments, as is still the case in France, Italy, and Germany, among others. Complete privatization of these utilities is another priority.

2. *Liberalization of the labor market*   Firing costs should be eliminated or at least vastly reduced and the role of judges in labor disputes vastly curtailed. Instead of stopping firms from firing workers they no longer need, unemployment subsidies should be designed to offer workers insurance in the event of spells of unemployment. These subsidies should be tied to actual job search and discontinued as soon as an unemployed worker refuses a job that he is deemed able to fulfill. Unemployment subsidies could be financed, in part, by charging firms a (moderate) tax on firings.

3. *Immigration*   The extreme solutions of complete openness and complete closure are unfeasible. The rational economic solution is selected immigration, as in the European Green Card proposal suggested by the Sapir Report. The criteria to use in issuing green cards should balance the needs of local labor markets and the potential social costs of immigration. As we discussed above, the risk is that governments may be captured by domestic interest groups and may not open up enough.

4. *Research and R&D*   To improve the system, more public money is not the point to start from. Universities should charge students for the cost of their education, setting some money aside to pay for scholarships. Government grants should only come in the form of scholarships to be used by students wherever they think they can get a good education. Making repayments of such grants conditional on the labor market outcome of the student, as recently adopted in the United Kingdom, is an idea to think about. Opaque, centralized hiring rules should be abolished, and each university should be free to hire whoever it likes and pay that person as much as it thinks he or she is worth. Universities should more actively seek private donations. The money used to pay for individual research grants could be assigned in the same way as the National Science Foundation in the United States assigns its grants. The Sapir Report also proposes this but does not resist the temptation to ask for additional public money. Instead, the funds could come from

the moneys saved by closing down the large national research centers and the Directorate for Research in the European Commission.

5. *Judicial systems and the cost of doing business*   The reasons why the cost of opening up a business is high differ from country to country. Solutions should therefore be found at the individual country levels. It is obvious that Italians cannot continue to have to spend 63 working days to open a business when in the United States it takes 4 days.

6. *Fiscal policy*   There are many critical aspects here. One is how to control budget deficits, a problem especially pressing for countries with large debt. This should be done quickly and by cutting spending by a few percentage points of GDP. Spending for public employment, public pensions, and various subsidies should be the targets of these cuts, even though the exact mix might vary country by country. Tax increases should not be used to achieve fiscal balance; on the contrary, spending cuts should be large enough to allow for reductions in the highest marginal tax rates. The European Central Bank could play an important role here. Rather than simply repeating, month after month, that governments should be more fiscally responsible, in its market operations the ECB could start discriminating among the bonds of fiscally sound and less fiscally sound countries. This simple change in the operating rules of the ECB would do more to bring about fiscal discipline than a complicated reform of the fine print of the Growth and Stability Pact. Cutting spending by a few percentage points of GDP does not mean that Europe should abandon its generous welfare state: one does not need a size of government equal to half of GDP to pay even for a generous welfare system. Most European countries face the rising cost of their pension systems and adverse demographic trends. Pension reforms cannot be postponed. The nature of such reforms will be quite different from one country to another.

In order to stop its decline, Europe does not need more government programs, more subsides for research and development, more
public money in infrastructures, more regulations, and more "pro-
growth" initiatives. Europe simply needs to put in place the right
incentives to invest, take risks, work, and do research. Growth will
follow. Europeans can avoid decline as long as they do not call for
"protection" from market challenges, but instead embrace them.

Index